Thank God It's Friday!

MEDITATIONS FOR HARDWORKING CATHOLICS

Thank God It's Friday!

MEDITATIONS FOR
HARDWORKING CATHOLICS

Andrew Costello

THE THOMAS MORE PRESS
Chicago, Illinois

ISBN-0-88347-213-9

Contents

PART THREE:
THE CLEANSING AND CLEARING OUT PROCESS

PART FOUR: THE PLANTING

TO MY BROTHER
WHO ANSWERED
"YES"
TO THE QUESTION,
"AM I MY BROTHER'S
KEEPER?"

INTRODUCTION

Thank God It's Friday.

It was Friday evening. I just got home from Maryland after seeing my brother for two days. He's slowly dying of melanoma—a deadly form of cancer. Last year, when they took a lump from near his left armpit, the doctor said it might show up elsewhere. It did. This year it's a tumor in his brain—left side again.

I'm dedicating this book to him, hoping it will be finished and published before he dies. He loves books.

On returning home there was a letter from Joel Wells, of the Thomas More Association, asking if I would put together a book called, "Thank God It's Friday: Meditations for Hardworking Catholics."

First reaction: "No way, Joel! I'm too busy already. And besides, I don't work on a Monday to Friday schedule."

Obviously, I changed my mind. This book is in your hands. What struck and what challenged me was the second sub-title that Joel put in his letter: "Spiritual Ideas for People with Busy Schedules."

That was me. Isn't that you too? We feel at times a call to a greater awareness of God, a deeper spirituality, holiness, wholeness, all those mysteries, while at the same time the phone rings, somebody gets sick, and there is so much to do.

Help!

Maybe this year I could try to squeeze into my schedule the writing of 52 meditations—one for every week or weekend. And maybe this year, you the reader, can fit into your schedule 52 meditations or spiritual themes. "Let's make a deal!"

That's the genesis, that's the format, and that's the hope of this book. I'll provide a reflection or meditation for every week or weekend of the year. Use them in what is your best quiet moment in the week for prayer and reflection.

9

The themes will be the basic ones of life—hoping that I'll grow by putting this book together and hoping you'll also grow in putting together the basic themes of your life.

At the end of each meditation, I'll provide a short mantra, or a mantra prayer, or a short quote, for your use all week. It's an old technique. The hope is that it will help keep the spiritual theme that I'm stressing before your mind.

One of the meditations that will be presented is called, "Rosary Beads Aren't Just for Hail Mary's Anymore" (Meditation 22). Dig out your rosary and keep it in your purse or everyday pocket and use it to repeat the mantra or quote at the end of each meditation a few thousand times that week.

Enough. Let's start this book. Let's begin this journey.

As Cardinal Suenens said, "To write a book is to make a journey into the unknown."

PART ONE
Conversion

Turning to Jesus who turns to us
and says, "Don't you realize there
are things about you that need to
be changed?"

1. ACCEPTING JESUS AS RABBI

THE most obvious place to begin a book on Christian spirituality
is to begin with Jesus.

It's so obvious that I once forgot Jesus in a dramatic way.

At the age of 44, after 24 years in a religious community called
"The Redemptorists," I was asked to be a novice master. The
job description would mainly be that of teaching new members
about our community, about prayer, and about the basics of religious life. I said "yes," knowing that it would stretch me. But
I also knew it would be like most jobs, something that I would
have to learn by doing and by asking around.

Luckily, I didn't have to work alone. There were two of us,
both new on the job. We were appointed to our combined novitiate
for Redemptorists from all over the United States. Our first class
numbered 23 men, ranging in age from 20 to 44. The place for
the novitiate was on the edge of a Wisconsin lake, with the beautiful
Indian name of Oconomowoc.

Gil Enderle, the other novice master, and I sat down and lined
up a whole year's course. We put on paper all the topics and themes
of spirituality and of the religious life that we thought were important. There was one exception: we left out Jesus.

Early in that first year, after floundering around for a while,
we hit a point when we wanted to give the novices a retreat: a
special period of prayer for four days.

11

We sat down, prayed, and then discussed what we thought should be covered during the retreat. Surprisingly, it hit us that we had left out Jesus. Of course, we referred to Jesus here and there, especially in our daily talks and sermons, etc., but as a major theme, no.

Lord have mercy. Christ have mercy. Lord have mercy.

So we prayed and then presented some basic reflections on Jesus. At the end of the year, some of the novices said that "the retreat on Jesus was the most important part of the year."

Jesus taught us that. The community taught us that. Thank God we were novice enough to learn that.

Jesus is Lord. Jesus is central. Jesus is the teacher of life.

Where is Jesus in your life? What place does he play? Would you be able to say in public that, "Jesus is the Lord of my life?" Or would you be scared, thinking that your friends would think you strange? Seriously, does Jesus play any role in your life? Or are you like I was, believing in Jesus, but not explicitly saying it?

After that first year on this job, our combined novitiate ended. This year I have the same job, still live near water, and this time it's with twelve novices in a beautiful building overlooking the Hudson River, at Esopus, New York.

That major learning about Jesus followed me, and I keep reflecting on Jesus as the one who can teach me about life. Perhaps, too, my title and my job as novice master help. I am learning that Jesus is the Master—Rabbi in Hebrew. I am learning that Jesus is a Teacher. That title of Jesus never hit me till I got this job. He is a master, I am a novice. And more and more I'm hearing in our daily liturgy, when the gospel is read, how often Jesus is called, "Rabbi," "Master" and "Teacher."

MANTRA PRAYER: *"Jesus, Rabbi, teach me the mysteries*
                     of life;
                     Jesus, Rabbi, be the Lord of my life."

2. ANDREW

IN my second year on this job, quite by accident I picked up a book, *A Meditator's Diary*, by Jane Hamilton-Merritt. I began reading it one Saturday afternoon and couldn't put it down. It was finished by 8:30 that evening.

It was the story of Jane Hamilton-Merritt's going to Thailand to study and experience first-hand a form of Buddhism called, "Therevada."

Great reading. She had worked in Southeast Asia, had gone to "wats" (temples), but it was always as an observer and as an outsider. She had read and studied quite a bit about Buddhism and Zen meditation, but she wanted an inside feel for it. Her hope was to go to Thailand and become a member of a community and study as a monk learning from a master, a teacher, abbot, or guru, whatever word you use.

Her book is divided into two parts. First she describes being accepted as a day student in a royal wat in Bangkok. In that temple she learned a form of meditation that brought her tranquility and inner peace. In that wat, and in another she also discovered in Bangkok, Jane began to study and understand Buddhism in depth. Part two of her book describes her journey to a remote Northern Thailand area where she actually lived in a wat. There she learned more about Buddhism and another form of meditation. The first one is called "Samadhi" or "Tranquility" meditation. In Northern Thailand she learned a second type "Vispassana" or "Wisdom" or "Insight" meditation. The first stressed breathing in the nostril area, the second down in the stomach area.

All this impressed me, probably because I'm learning to be a spiritual teacher. Here was someone with a great desire to learn from a master or abbot.

In my prayer and reflections on the New Testament I was finding myself approaching Jesus in the same posture as Jane. I too

13

wanted to hear first hand. Jesus as Rabbi was making more and more sense to me.

I began telling our novices to approach Jesus as the Master. I often said, "Don't make me the issue. Make Jesus the issue." Even though I had the title of "master," I kept saying "Jesus is the Teacher. Jesus is the Rabbi."

Does that title for Jesus hit you? Have you ever thought of approaching Jesus as a Rabbi and a teacher?

To many Christians, the thought of having any kind of relationship with Jesus doesn't even cross their mind. Jesus seems further away than some spiritual teacher or guru in some remote wat in Northern Thailand. To many Catholics, the Pope is made central and Jesus as person doesn't enter their consciousness. And many people got upset when the Beatles said they were better known than Jesus Christ.

Recently, I picked up the Gospel of John and a scene from the first chapter hit me. One day Andrew and one of his friends were standing on the planet, and Jesus walked by. John the Baptist, also standing there, pointed him out to Andrew and his friend: "Look, there is the Lamb of God!" It must have hit Andrew because he began following Jesus. Noticing what was happening, Jesus stopped and asked, "What are you looking for?"

And they answered, "Rabbi, where do you stay?"

And Jesus said, "Come and see!"

And after staying with Jesus that day, Andrew rushed home to tell his brother Simon, "We have found the Messiah."

Notice what happened to Andrew: Jesus had switched from Rabbi to Messiah after only one afternoon of listening to him.

And Andrew brought Simon to Jesus.

And in time Simon switched from Simon the fisher of fish to Peter the fisher of people.

Isn't that a great thing to do for someone: to bring them to Jesus? I, Andrew, want to bring you by means of this book to Jesus. And you too will be challenged to change. You too will receive a deeper call and a newer vision for your life.

And Jesus is not in some remote cloud in heaven, nor in some remote monastery in Thailand.

"Look, there is the Lamb of God!"

MANTRA PRAYER: *"Rabbi, where do you stay?"*
                              "Come and see."

3. I'VE BEEN TO THE MOUNTAIN

YEARS ago I remember hearing a story or fable that went somewhat like this.

Once upon a time there was a man who wanted to know the secret of happiness and the meaning of life.

So he traveled all over the world talking to gurus, teachers, philosophers, religious leaders, anybody and everybody he thought would give him the secret of happiness and the meaning of life. India, China, Sri Lanka, California, Africa, remote islands—you name them, he was there. He was a searcher.

But no answer satisfied him. Sitting in a bar in Brooklyn, depressed, almost broke, he told the bartender his story, how he had searched everywhere for a teacher who would give him the secret of happiness and the meaning of life.

"Well, when I was in Vietnam," the bartender told him, "I heard there was an old wise man in Tibet, who lived in a cave, high up on a mountain, who knows the secret of happiness and the meaning of life."

The man, till that moment depressed and burnt out, jumped up, paid for his drink and ran out the door, screaming "Thank you! Thank you."

He sold the very little he had left, gathered up all the money that he could get, and headed for Tibet.

Finally, after traveling and searching for about six months, he found out where the old wise man lived. He climbed the mountain. Cut, tired, he came upon the old man who was sitting outside his cave facing the setting sun.

"Great teacher," he began, "thank God I found you. I've been searching all over the world for the secret of happiness and the meaning of life. I've been to India, China, Sri Lanka, I've been to California, I've been to many remote islands. I almost gave up till a bartender in Brooklyn told me that you have the secret of happiness and the meaning of life."

17

The old man smiled. "Yes, I have the secret of happiness and the meaning of life."

"What is it?"

"Life is a river, without a beginning or an end, that flows both ways."

Seeing the stunned look on his visitor's face, the old wise man of the mountain said, "That's it! That's the secret!"

And the searcher said, "Do you mean to say I came all the way here to Tibet, after selling every last thing I had, and you're telling me that the secret of happiness and the meaning of life is, "Life is a river without a beginning or an end, that flows both ways?"

And the old wise man said, "You mean it isn't?"

The end of the story.

What is the secret of happiness? What is the meaning of life?

If you knew that there was a great teacher somewhere in the world, would you go to listen to that teacher? If you could talk to that person one to one, would you drop everything you're doing now and go to him or her with your questions about life?

Does the idea grab you? Are you a searcher, a pilgrim, someone who wants to know what life and happiness are all about?

Wait a minute. Pause. Stop reading this book for a minute. Where are you?

Questions: *Has anything I said so far hit you? Are you where you are reading these pages or are you somewhere else?*

Jesus came to people where they were—Matthew in his tax office; James and John at the dock on the Lake of Galilee. Or people came to Jesus and Jesus listened to where they were: Nicodemus in the dark night of his soul; the woman at the well living on the surface of her life, afraid to go down into the deep waters of her heart.

If people don't even listen to themselves how can they listen to Jesus?

Jesus is a great wisdom teacher. Have you ever really listened and thought about what he's saying?

Get a tape recorder and get a Bible. Slowly read into the tape recorder Chapters 5-6-7 of Matthew. It's the Sermon on the Mount. Leave a little silence in between each new saying or each new image or thought.

Next, find a quiet place where you can be alone. Picture yourself going to listen to a great teacher who is going to teach you about life and meaning.

Dim the lights, have a candle lit, sit quietly, relax. Then when you are ready to listen, start the tape. Use the pause button or shut off the machine after each saying or when something that Jesus said in the Sermon on the Mount strikes you.

Then reflect upon what Jesus is saying.

Where in the world can you hear teachings as good as those of Jesus the Rabbi, Jesus the Master, Jesus the Teacher?

In Thailand, Jane Hamilton-Merritt discovered that the Buddha gave the great teaching that life is filled with "dukkha," meaning suffering, unhappiness and hurt, and that one of the secrets of happiness and life is "sukkha," which means the elimination of all desires. The Buddha would teach you to meditate and concentrate on how everything around us is always decaying and wearing out. Get rid of desires and wanting to control relationships, situations and things, and you will be much more at peace.

Doesn't Jesus say the same thing in his Sermon on the Mount? "Do not lay up for yourselves an earthly treasure. Moths and rust corrode, thieves break in and steal. Make it your practice instead to store up heavenly treasures, which neither moths nor rust corrode nor thieves break in and steal. Remember where your treasure is, there your heart is also" (Matthew 6:19-21).

Climb the mountain and listen to the sermons of Jesus. Let him preach the Sermon on the Mount to you personally, one to one.

One of the strongest arguments for Jesus is his clearness of thought and depth of ideas. He is both clear water and deep water.

And the Sermon on the Mount is only one collection of the teachings of Jesus from the early Church. Start there and then read his parables, especially in Luke, and then his poetry, especially in John. Slowly savoring his words you'll experience the wisdom of a great teacher, Jesus the Rabbi.

Go to the mountain. Spend time with the Rabbi. Listen to his secrets of happiness and meanings about life.

Like Martin Luther King, Jr., you'll come down from the mountain with the meaning. You'll come down with a vision. You too will have a dream. You'll come down with more than, "Life is a river, without a beginning or an end, that flows both ways."

MANTRA: *"I've been to the mountain."*

4. THE FIRST TEACHING: CONVERSION—ME FIRST

THE first teaching of Jesus is the call and the challenge to change. That's the doorway into the Kingdom where one can experience happiness because one is living the meaning of life: giving. On this one, Jesus does not fish for us, trying to catch us with a parable. He comes right out and tells it like it is: "Repent! Change! The Kingdom of Heaven is now. I'm calling you to a whole new way of thinking, a whole new way of feeling, a whole new way of living, a whole new way of dying."

I remember going to see the movie, "The Gospel According to St. Matthew," a film by Paulo Pier Pasolini. It was a stark, blunt life of Jesus, without the cuteness or the music or the frills of "Godspell" or "Jesus Christ Superstar."

Right from the opening scene I sat up. There was Jesus on the black and white screen calling for changes and I was ready. There was Jesus walking up a road and there were some people walking down the same road. Jesus stops and megaphones his hands, "Reform your lives. The Kingdom of God is at hand" (Matthew 4:14).

I was so impressed by that movie and that call to change and conversion that I left the theater and did what so many people do when they are hit by the message of conversion. I went home and tried to convert somebody else. This priest in our community was drunk most of the time, so I pushed him to come with me the next day to see this great movie about Jesus. "It will help you with your preaching!"

The next day, there I was sitting in the movie theater with this guy. Like Andrew, I was going to bring him to Jesus. Being 27 and naive, I wasn't aware that this was not to be his moment for conversion.

The movie began. Once more I was impressed by the stark, black and white scenes and the stark, black and white words, "Reform

21

your lives. The Kingdom of God is at hand.''

I looked over to the priest next to me to see if he was getting conversion. And there he was fast asleep.

That was a conversion moment for me.

And the conversion was the insight that conversion is for me. Jesus' words hit me, ''Why do you see the speck in your brother's eye and miss the plank in your own?''

Conversion is for me.

Repent! Change! Reform my life. The Kingdom of God is at hand for me.

Conversion is for the person in my seat, in my skin, in my skull.

In that conversion experience, I didn't cry like St. Augustine in his big experience in the garden in Milan. I didn't fall to the ground and hear voices from God like St. Paul on the road to Damascus. No, I was in a movie theater, in the dark, next to a sleeping, alcoholic priest, and I began to laugh at myself. I saw myself as I really was at the age of 27: young, stupid, naive, and wondering.

It was an awakening, but not a ''rude awakening'' like many conversions are.

However, like most conversion moments, it came when I least expected it. Obviously, moments of grace, moments of conversion, can't be planned, scheduled or programmed. It was a teachable moment. I was ready to see myself as I was, plus, I was able to laugh or cry.

There's the key: the teachable moment. A priest I know loves ''hospital work,'' because the teachable moments are many. And the key people are not just the people who are sick or dying. Often they are the people around the bed or out in the hall waiting and watching and wondering.

The teachable moment is the moment we can't control. It's the moment when we admit we can't do it all. It's the moment when Augustine and Paul knew they hit bottom and had lost control. They were on the ground looking down. It was either the grave, ongoing non-living, or conversion.

As Jesus said, "Everyone who exalts himself shall be humbled and he who humbles himself shall be exalted!" (Luke 14:11).

The teachable moment is the moment I realize I can't do it. I need a power greater than myself. But we're like kids in shop class, unable to say to the person next to us or the teacher, "I need help. I don't know what to do. I don't know how this works."

Paul cried out, "Who are you?" And he found out that the power greater than himself was the power he was trying to destroy: Jesus Christ.

Augustine in his teachable moment cried out, "How long, how long? Tomorrow and tomorrow?" For years he kept putting off conversion. For years he let the power of sin control him. He was his own center. In his inner dialogue he heard questions like: "Do you think these young people who are living a chaste life are doing it on their own power?" "Why are you trying to stand on your own strength and keep falling?" "Why don't you rely on God like they are?" Then he heard a voice in the garden say "Take and read. Take and read." So he picked up the letter of Paul to the Romans and read those great conversion words, "Let us live honorably as in daylight; not in carousing and drunkeness, not in sexual excess and lust, not in quarreling and jealousy. Rather put on the Lord Jesus Christ and make no provisions for the desires of the flesh" (Romans 13:13-14).

MANTRA: *Here I am Lord, help me to be ready*
when my conversion moments come.

5. FOUR TYPES OF PEOPLE

ONE afternoon, Jesus, aged 21, decided to quit work early and go out for a hike into the countryside.

He left Nazareth and walked about three miles to one of his favorite spots. It was on a hill, under a tree, overlooking an enormous field. In the distance he could see Nazareth.

In the field that afternoon was a farmer sowing seed. For the past five Fridays Jesus had seen him digging, and plowing, preparing for this moment. They often waved to each other. The farmer, about ten years older, saw Jesus as a nice carpenter, but rather quiet.

The farmer seemed to love his work and especially this moment, tossing the seed in all directions.

Jesus sat there enjoying it all—especially the bread and wine that he had brought with him. He had told Mary that he'd be back around sunset.

The farmer finished. As he was heading home for supper he waved to Jesus and Jesus to him.

Jesus watched him all the way back to his house. Then Jesus jumped up. He was waiting for this moment. He wanted to see everything up close. Mary was often intrigued how he stopped in the marketplace to look at wineskins and cloaks, yeast and salt. She turned all these things over in her heart as he turned mustard seeds over and over in his hand.

Standing in the middle of the field, Jesus saw the seeds sitting everywhere in the soil below—in the mountains and in the valleys of the furrows he was standing on and in. Then he walked to the edge of the field. He noticed with sadness that some seed landed amongst the thorn bushes that lined the edge of the field.

On his way back to the road he noticed some seed scattered on soil that just didn't look right. So he got a stick and poked below the soil. He was right. He hit rock almost immediately. Did the farmer know about this shallow soil? Jesus didn't. After all he

was just a carpenter. Or did the farmer let the seed land here for
the birds? Wouldn't that be nice if that's the way life worked?
Jesus wondered and then turned quickly. Sure enough there were
birds, but they were all in the middle of the field having a feast.
Jesus laughed as he headed back to the road. He stopped. There
on the road all along the edge of the field were seeds. The wind
must have taken them there or the farmer was having a good year.
As he walked along the road he felt strange, stepping on all those
seeds.

Then he got a bright idea. He checked. Nobody could be seen
at the farmer's house. And nobody else was in sight. So Jesus took
off his cloak. Next he went and got some bushes and made a crude
broom. He began sweeping up all the seeds he could from along
the road. Then he put them in his cloak.

When he finished sweeping the whole road, he had a whole sack
of seeds and soil. Once more he walked into the middle of the
field, where he saw the birds had finished their feast. He took
the seed and played farmer, and tossed it in all directions. The
seed landed on good soil.

It was almost sunset, so Jesus got moving. Mary knew him by
now. He often got back after dark.

Ten years later, Jesus was preaching in the same area. He looked
out at the crowd who had come to hear him preach, he looked
into their eyes, looking into their hungers. He stopped. There was
the farmer. He had heard that Jesus, the carpenter, of all people,
had become Jesus the Rabbi. Jesus waved to him and gave him
a nice smile as if it was only yesterday afternoon that he was in
his field.

And Jesus began speaking: "Open your ears like a field ready
to receive seed."

Everyone, especially the farmer, were all ears at that opening
comment of Jesus.

"Once upon a time there was a farmer who went out sowing
in his field. Some seeds landed on the footpath, where the birds
came along and ate the seeds up. Some seed landed on rocky

ground, where it had little soil. It sprouted up immediately and
died immediately, because the sun scorched it and it withered because it had no roots. And some seed landed amongst the thorns.
When they grew up, they were choked off and there was no yield
of grain. But the seed that landed on good soil, yielded grain that
sprang up to produce at a rate of thirty, sixty or a hundred fold.''

Then Jesus ended with the words, ''Let those who have ears
to hear, hear!''

The farmer sat there amazed. Jesus seemed to have talked just
to him. And then the second thoughts began hitting him. And for
months and years afterward, he and his family and friends discussed
what Jesus had said. They ended up with about three or four in-
terpretations. They would laugh, because rabbi's were famous for
doing that.

Ten years later, a few of Jesus' disciples were in the area preaching. Naturally the farmer went to hear them.

Surprise: once more he heard the Parable of the Sower. But this
time, the farmer spoke up, ''What does the Parable mean?''

And the disciple said that they had asked Jesus that same question. And then they told the farmer and his friends what Jesus
meant.

''Some people don't hear a word you are saying. They are like
the road, as deaf as stone. When the word hits them, nothing happens. They are too wrapped up in evil. The Devil runs their life.
They are the people Jesus meant when he said some seed landed
on the road and the birds of the air eat it up, or people walking
on the road trample it down.

''Next come the people who are like the seed that lands on
shallow soil and it quickly starts to grow and quickly starts to die.
They are the people who have loud conversions. They hear the
word of God and take it to heart with joy. But as soon as any problem, or pressure, or stress hits them, they are back to being their
shallow selves.

''And some people are good soil. But they have too many things going on in their lives. They are like the seed that lands in the weeds which choke off the word. Anxieties about this, worries about that, the desires for this, and the craving for that, choke it off and the seed yields nothing.

"And then there are people who are the good soil. They hear the word of God; they take it to heart; they yield grain thirty, sixty and a hundred fold."

The farmer smiled. That's what he thought Jesus meant. And for the rest of his life, whenever he stood in the field ready for the moment of tossing seed, he would first turn and look to the spot where Jesus sat. He would then look in all directions to make sure nobody saw him. Then he would wave to Jesus and start tossing his seed.

MANTRA QUESTION: *Which of the four am I?*

6. THE FIELD

THE field then is an image that Jesus loved to use. Come to think about it, for a carpenter, he seems to have been far more interested in farm work and fields.

Still, there are a few carpenter images. He urged people to come through the narrow door. The wide door that everybody takes doesn't lead to life. He ends the Sermon on the Mount by warning everyone to build their life on his words. That would be equivalent to building one's house on rock rather than sand. In the Gospel of Luke he gets more descriptive, talking about making sure one digs deep enough so that the foundations of one's life will be on rock.

Everyone knows Jesus' teaching about not seeing specks in one's neighbors' eyes while missing the plank in one's own. Did that idea come to him in the carpenter shop, where he got a speck in his eye while watching his neighbor?

And on the way to the cross, seeing some women crying, Jesus muttered, "If they do these things in the green wood, what will happen in the dry?"

And as carpenter, he died with and on the things of his trade: hammer, nails, wood.

But it was the fields that Jesus constantly referred to in his teaching and in his thoughts. Read the Gospels. See the images and pictures that he's talking about: farmers, shepherds, pig herders, pigs, foxes, sheep, goats, wolves, birds, oxen, vineyards, wheat, weeds, mustard trees, fig trees, fruit trees, good trees, bad trees. He talks about putting the ax to the root and one's hand to the plow. And he warns those who accept the plow, "If you keep looking back, you're not fit for the Kingdom of God." You'll also have a crooked row. He refers to wheat ground down to flour, then mixed with yeast to become bread. And we need wine with bread, so he talked about grapes being crushed into wine. And he stressed: make sure you don't ruin new wine or old wine; put the new wine in new wine skins and the old wine into old wine skins.

So Jesus knew all about the fields and the products of the fields. Where did he learn all this? "Is this not the carpenter's son?" Evidently Jesus didn't just cut wood and build houses during his first thirty years. He who made doors knew a lot about the great outdoors. He warned a scribe who wanted to follow him: "The foxes have lairs, the birds of the sky have nests, but the Son of Man has nowhere to lay his head" (Luke 8:20).

One of the first things we must do after a conversion experience, is to take time out and look at our field. A good image is that of Jesus, sitting under a tree on a hill, overlooking a field, watching a farmer sow seed.

We need to take time out to see what's going on in the field of our life. We need to see where the good soil is and where the shallow soil is, to see where the roads are and where the weeds are.

I am the farmer sowing seed, but I can also be Jesus sitting there watching and wondering about what's going on in front of me, the daily business of my life.

In the next section of this book, Part Two, I'll give a lot more on this important step in the spiritual life, that of stepping back and looking at what is going on in my life.

It's enough to say here that each of us needs to make three important statements about ourselves.

1. I am a field and there have been a lot of things planted in my life.

2. I am my field, and things have happened in that field for better or for worse, and I can't separate myself from that reality till death do me part.

3. There is a treasure in this field called me, otherwise God would not have created me.

These three statements will be covered in the next three chapters.

MANTRA PRAYER: *"Take off your shoes,
you are standing on holy ground"
(Exodus 3:5).*

7. WHAT'S PLANTED IN YOUR FIELD

DIG anywhere and you'll always find dirt.

No wonder people are scared to enter into politics or public life. There are things in our private life that we don't want known in our public life.

Dig anywhere and you'll always find dirt.

Everybody has skeletons in their closets and dead bones in their field.

There are also treasures in our field, but what we're worried about is the truth.

Imagine if someone could see right into us and know everything we have ever done. Imagine if there were no fig leafs or shower curtains or towels to grab to hide our inner nakedness.

Should we keep digging up the past or should we let sleeping bones lie?

If they have neither been forgiven nor forgotten, then I think they need to be looked at. You be the judge, or let whoever you talk to as your closest friend or counselor be the judge. Get a second opinion.

Write down (and then rip up) the five worst things that you have ever done, experiences that you want to keep hidden forever. Write down in another column (and then rip up) the five worst things that were done to you. And is there anything you are doing now that you are ashamed of, behavior you would not want on page one, or any page, of the local newspaper?

Dig anywhere and you'll always find dirt.

Dig anywhere and you'll always find treasures.

Often we hide the treasures not only from those around us, but also from ourselves. Then we go through life concentrating most of our energies on the negative.

And we don't stop at death. We go through life worried about the great accounting at the end of the world after our death. Jesus' words scare us: "There is nothing that is concealed that will not

31

be revealed, nothing hidden that will not become known" (Matthew 10:26).

Those strong words of Jesus have scared a lot of people away from sin and from messing up their life. The fear of hell often motivates better than the desire for heaven. Unfortunately, fear is stronger than love.

The only relief is knowing that the great revelation will take place after we're all dead and we'll all be in the same field together, sheep and goats.

That image of the great judgment in the 25th chapter of Matthew always gives me a feeling of helplessness. I get a glimpse of it before going into seeing the doctor or the dentist for an examination. I always fear what they might find because of my not taking care of my teeth or my health. I also get a strange feeling, when I see documentary films of World War II, in which they show scenes of naked men and women of the Holocaust, being led like sheep to the slaughter—either to the gas chambers or into some field to be shot.

"Make an accounting of your stewardship." What's planted in your garden? Why do you ignore the treasure and concentrate on the trash?

We concentrate on the trash and then concentrate on keeping it hidden. That's how evil, evil is.

We are like people caught doing something wrong and who have to show up at the courthouse for a hearing or a trial. They cover their faces from the cameras and the reporters. They run out the door and down the steps trying to hide behind a coat, hat, newspaper, anything they can use to cover their shame.

St. Paul, St. Augustine, C. S. Lewis, and many other great spiritual writers, all try to get us to see that it's better to walk in the light than sneak in the night.

In the conversion process we need to make full disclosure. We demand it of our politicians but not for ourselves. Imagine if twenty dollar bills, motel walls, interiors of cars, telephones, and back rooms could talk.

And, Jesus adds, that is only the beginning. Externals are nothing compared to our internal thoughts and desires. Often we are good only because we're afraid of being caught. We keep the outside of the cup clean because of our neighbor, for show, to protect our reputation. Jesus is concerned with the inside story. "What emerges from within a person, that and nothing else makes them impure. Wicked designs come from the deep recesses of the heart: acts of fornication, theft, murder, adulterous conduct, greed, maliciousness, deceit, sensuality, envy, blasphemy, arrogance, an obtuse spirit. All these evils come from within and render a person impure" (Mark 7: 21-22).

All that is too much to face. No wonder we'd rather keep it and ourselves in the dark.

Jesus walks down our road, our street, and every once and a while he says, "Face it! If you don't, you won't see how it's killing you."

And not only are our deep, dark, unacknowledged sins killing us, we are killing others because of them.

Now Jesus knows we all have skeletons in our closets, alligators in our basements, and dead bones in our field. He knew Ezechiel's prophecy about all the people of Israel being a field of dead bones.

What did Jesus see when he looked at people? Did he see people as we see people? Did he walk around and see people as dead bones? Poets and prophets see differently.

What does Jesus see when he sees us? We are so self-centered that we probably think he looks at us the same way we look at ourselves, that he judges us as we judge ourselves. We block out the Gospel story that Jesus looked at people with pity and sorrow, crying because they were dead. We block out the Gospel story that Jesus saw people with love and hoped that they would change and come back to life.

So conversion means allowing ourselves to see ourselves as we really are: treasure and trash.

So conversion means allowing Jesus to challenge us to use our gifts, treasures and talents in new ways and to stop blocking those gifts because of our trash and sins.

So conversion means allowing Jesus to heal us, beginning with a confession, beginning with an open admission that I need help. I can't do it alone. I need help in facing and dealing with my trash.

In recent years it was probably Alcoholics Anonymous and Carl Jung who did the most to stress this need of acknowledging our sinful and shadow side. In fact, if we go through life unwilling to admit our sins, we'll end up doing what Jesus hoped we wouldn't do, "Let him without sin throw the first stone."

Throwing stones, projecting our motives and garbage onto others, brings us right back to Jesus' teaching about seeing specks in our neighbor's eye and missing the plank in our own.

Blame the other person. Make the Communists the bad guys. Make women the source of temptation. Make fun of minorities. Stand taller by trying to lower other people or by stepping on them. We have hundreds of tricks hidden in our shadows, if we want to avoid looking at the toxic waste dumped in our own field.

Jesus didn't come to embarrass us. He didn't come to make us cemetaries. He came to make us fields of wheat—resurrection fields. He came to make us gardens of delight where we can work at peace with each other and enjoy the Lord in the cool of the evening, without having to hide in the bushes naked and ashamed of our day.

MANTRA: *"Dig anywhere and you'll always find dirt."*

8. WHEAT AND WEEDS

SO we have to see and we have to admit, that we have both wheat and weeds in our yard. Everybody has both. Those who admit to only wheat or only weeds are unbalanced. Check it out: they are probably the people who drive us crazy.

"Once upon a time," Jesus, the Rabbi, said, "there was a farmer who sowed good seed in his field. Then one night, when everyone was asleep, an enemy came to the farmer's field and sowed poisonous darnel *(lolium temulentum)*, a weed which in its early stages of growth looks like wheat. A while later, when his farm hands saw the weeds growing with the wheat they rushed to the farmer. 'Didn't you sow good seed in your field?' Then they added before the farmer could say, 'Yes,' that there were weeds all through his field along with his wheat. Then the farmer yelled, 'An enemy has done this!' His farm hands then asked, 'Should we go and pull up the weeds?' 'No,' replied the farmer, 'if you pull up the weeds, you'll pull up the wheat with them. Let them both grow till harvest. Then we'll collect the weeds and burn them and the wheat we'll gather for my barns.' "

According to the Bible specialist, Joachim Jeremias, who gives the comment about the poisonous darnel in his book, *The Parables of Jesus,* the story refers to the Last Judgment at the end of the world. Then the good will be separated from the bad, like wheat from weeds, like sheep from goats. The good will go to heaven and the bad will go to hell.

However, it dawned on me that we can also use the parable as an allegory about personal growth: development and mal-development.

Picture the grey brain inside the skull as a field. As we develop, especially in the springtime of our life, wheat and weeds are planted in our brain. Parents, television, tapes, radio, sisters, brothers, aunts, uncles, teachers, friends, enemies, all plant both good and bad seeds in our brain. When we're young, we're more impressionable. Unfortunately, some kids are abused or neglected or treated unfairly and those seeds, those memories, remain with them all their life. They might learn to forgive, but they can't forget—especially those who were severely abused.

In an open forum I once heard a man in his 60's tell about an incident in his childhood. He was sitting at the kitchen table with his older brother and his dad. He was in the sixth grade; his brother was about to graduate from the eighth grade. And his dad began telling his older brother, "You're going to go to the best high school in the city. You're going to get a good education and then you'll go to college. Then you'll go to medical or law school. You'll end up a great doctor or lawyer." And the younger brother asked, "And what about me, dad? What about me?" And turning, with a scowl on his face, his father pointing to his shoe said, "You! You have less brains than the sole of my shoe. You'll never amount to anything." Then there was a big pause in the room. With tears coming down his face, the man lowered his head, and told us, "My father was right. I never amounted to anything."

An enemy has done this.

And sometimes we have nobody to blame but ourselves. Sometimes we are our own worst enemy, because of the garbage and dangerous waste we plant in our brain. As they say in computer classes, "Garbage in; garbage out." Watch enough junk television programs, read enough poor novels, look at enough pornography, vegetate on enough mindless conversations over the phone or over a bar, and our field will be filled with weeds that we ourselves allowed to be planted. We become what we eat. We become what we read, see and hear. We become what we plant.

Now, is there anything that we can do to change past situations before we die? Do we have to continue to be victims of crimes we committed in the past or hurts that were done to us?

I've thought about this a lot and I believe that Jesus gave us an insight that he didn't plan to give when he told the story of the wheat and the weeds. Is he telling us that we do damage to ourselves if we try to go through life trying to remove weeds that can't be removed? If we made our life a waste dump or someone else dumped on us, then we might have to live with permanent damage all through our life.

The script is to get help, if we need help. We can get counseling or join a self-help group like Alanon or Adult Children of Alcoholics or an Incest Survivors Group, etc.

We all know the story of the man who kept writing to the government for advice on how to get rid of dandelions. Each suggestion they sent him was tried and each one failed. Their last suggestion was, "Learn to live with them."

The handicapped person must learn to live not only with the handicap, but also with the memories associated with it. Acceptance is the first step. So many people go through life with cuts from their childhood or later that never become scars. They keep picking the cut. They keep trying to bring up bad memories to make themselves feel bad. They think that's the way to get back at someone who hurt them. They don't realize that the opposite is true. Holding onto hurts, hurts the one who is holding onto them more than the one they are trying to hurt by holding onto them. Scars are better than open cuts. Scars are tough cuts. Scars are reminders that we have been hurt or cut there, but they are also reminders that we have been healed there.

Jesus, the Rabbi, teaches that we can be healed. Jesus, the Rabbi, teaches that we all have sinned and have been sinned against. Jesus, the Rabbi, teaches forgiveness. He doesn't tell us that we have to forget. But he does teach us to say from the cross of hurt, "Father, forgive them, for they don't know what they are doing."

Our past then can help us to learn forgiveness. Our past can help us to deal with the future. Our past hurts and sins can help us to understand others. We know what it is to have sinned and to have been sinned against. Obviously, it's a horrible way to learn compassion and understanding. It's an education degree that nobody wants to receive. It's too expensive. Abuse, rejection, and being hurt, especially when a child, is not the education one would want to receive, but if it happened, then let's hope people can learn in time to deal with the pain, especially with understanding and forgiveness.

And after acceptance and recognition then there is time for a cut to become a scar.

MANTRA: *"Father forgive them, for they didn't know what they were doing."*
or *"Father forgive me, for I didn't know what I was doing."*

9. THERE IS A TREASURE IN YOUR FIELD

MUCH of what has been said so far is the negative side of conversion: looking at the weeds. The other half of the conversion process is the positive side: looking at the wheat.

To be converted, we can't just look at hell, we also have to see heaven. But as indicated, most have to go to hell before they want to go to heaven.

Once upon a time Jesus gave a very simple example: "The Kingdom of God is like a buried treasure which a man found in a field. He hid it again, and rejoicing at his find went and sold all that he had and bought that field" (Matthew 13:44).

What's the treasure? Silver? Gold? A box of coins? A well? What is it?

It's part of the folk literature of so many cultures that the treasure is already in our ownership. It's our family. It's in our own backyard. It's our home. It's us. We have all read the folk stories of people searching the whole world over, only to find happiness in themselves, in their own backyard.

What's the treasure? Suppose we tell somebody there is a treasure in a field. They might buy or rent the latest metal detector or an oil drill or whatever equipment they need to try to find the treasure. And suppose the treasure is the field itself—not as it is, but what we can make it. Suppose it would make a great location for a store or a service station and nobody realized it? Don't people describe an ice cream store in the right spot as a "gold mine"?

To be converted we need to dream. To change we have to have a vision of something better. Isn't that the pitch of every advertisement? Isn't that the promise Moses gave his people? Otherwise they would rather have remained slaves in Egypt. Isn't that the promise held out to immigrants?

I think it was Sam Levenson who used to tell a story that went something like this. Our parents and grandparents, when they were on the other side, were told that the streets of America were paved with gold. When they arrived here they found out that the streets were not only not paved with gold, they weren't even paved. And, surprise! They had to pave them. There it is, the conversion process in a nutshell. We need the dream and we need to work to realize the dream.

And the temptation is to give up and want to return home when we find out we're in a desert or the streets aren't paved with gold, or aren't even paved. It takes a lot of work to reach the Promised Land.

In the 1960's, when I was a parish priest on the lower east side in New York, all was paved with cement and macadam—except for some abandoned lots. These lots were ugly spots—empty fields filled with broken bottles, old mattresses, abandoned cars without windows, doors, or hoods, metal carcasses that kids, like scavenger birds, slowly pulled apart for fun.

Most of us saw these lots as disaster areas and did nothing. But some people saw them as a treasure in their midst. Cutting through city red tape, getting garbage trucks and friends, they would have a big Saturday cleanup. Sometimes they made them into a playing field for kids, getting lights and setting up a basketball court and also a few benches for old people. And sometimes they worked on restoring the earth, digging it, watering it, fertilizing it. In time, grass, vegetables, trees and flowers were planted. Surprised, people passing by would crack a smile and make nice comments, seeing things growing on their street.

In the last meditation I stressed that there are some things that can't be changed. As the serenity prayer puts it, those are the things we need to learn to accept. In this meditation the stress is on the other part of the serenity prayer, to have the courage to change the things that I can change. Obviously, we need to pray for the wisdom to know the difference.

Some things can change. Some weeds can be pulled. Some garbage can be removed. This is the classical purgative way. People can change. People who play the same tape over and over and over again, can remove the tape and play some new songs. We don't have to keep repeating ourselves. It makes for a boring marriage, vacation or meeting if people know what we're going to say before we open our mouths. We can throw away our old script and write a new one for our time on the stage of life. Transactional Analysis and other therapies spell this out loud and clear. We can challenge each other to grow, telling each other, "Let's breathe some fresh air into our relationships and into our meetings. Let's stop playing all these boring games we know we're playing with each other."

And what about all those people in our life whom we hope will change. Can we do anything to change them? We work with people, we pray with people, we live with people, we are married to people, we can't stand or understand any more. There are people who bother us, who sin against us (those famous "trespass against us" folks). They make strange noises, they eat differently, they lick the spoon to clean it before putting it in the sugar bowl, they are always late, they are always talking sports or diets, they take our parking spots, they are always on the phone, they don't bag their garbage, they spend too much time on their coffee breaks or not enough time, they are too fat or too skinny, they drive us up the wall when we ride in a car with them. We all have our lists of things and people we would love to see changed.

In my book, *How to Deal with Difficult People,* I should have stressed even more that the main person who has to change in dealing with difficult people is me, not them. That's where the conversion needs to take place. If we can communicate and help each other change, great; if we can't, we have to learn to live with the dandelions and the weeds.

Kurt Lewin, a psychologist, famous for his idea of seeing social situations as a field of forces, as in a magnetic field, stressed that one change in the field forces changes in the whole field.

So, in the conversion process, if we change, the whole house, the whole office, the whole field we live in changes.

The stress Jesus makes is starting with oneself. Ask yourself, "Where in the neighborhood called me is there a spot, a lot, a field, where I can change? Start small. Dream. Turn a disaster area into a gold mine.

MANTRA: *The Kingdom of God is like a treasure buried in my field.*

10. THE GOLDEN BRIDGE

BEFORE I move on to the second part of this book, "Helps in the Conversion Process," I would like to sum up the first section on "Conversion" with the image of "The Golden Bridge."

A man who was working on a weight problem once told me excitedly about the image of "The Golden Bridge." His therapist gave it to him. He said it really helped him and maybe I could use it to help other people.

I've used it on myself and presented it in talks. It's the basic "Before and After" technique used in so many advertisements. Its strength lies in that it's easy to picture or imagine.

Picture a golden bridge. On the land on the right side of the bridge all is good; on the land on the left side of the bridge all is bad.

If you want to lose weight, he told me, picture yourself on the right side of the bridge: thin, happy, eating the right foods, exercising, enjoying life in a balanced and happy way.

And everytime you "pig out," everytime you give up and load up on calories because you're angry or frustrated or for reasons unknown, then you've crossed the golden bridge and you've gone back to your old neighborhood.

The image is as simple as that.

Heaven or hell? Egypt or the Promised Land? A lot filled with broken bottles, old mattresses and destroyed cars or a spot for grass, flowers, a nice bench and a basketball court?

It's the image of Psalm I. Do I want to be like a tree planted near running water that yields fruit in due season, and whose leaves never fade, and whatever I do prospers? Or do I want to be just the opposite, to be like empty chaff which the wind blows away? The choice is mine.

It's the message that Jesus gives in a dozen images: wheat or weeds, sheep or goats, good tree or bad, house on rock or house on sand, wide road or narrow road? The choice is always mine.

43

It's the message of Paul in the fifth chapter of his letter to the Galatians when he talks about the choice of living by the spirit or by the flesh. Using the image of the bridge, on the left is his list of what proceeds from living by the flesh or one's lower nature; on the right of the bridge is what results from living by one's higher nature—the spirit. What follows is his list, lined up in two columns. Which side describes you better? Which side of the bridge do you want to live on? Which neighborhood do you prefer? The choice is always yours.

lewd conduct	love
impurity	joy
sensuality	peace
idolatry	patient endurance
witchcraft	kindness
hatred	generosity
bickering	faith
jealousy	tolerance
outbursts of rage	and chastity
selfish rivalry	
dissentions	
factions	
envy	
drunkenness	
orgies and the like	

Notice that Paul's list has more negatives than positives. Is he too pessimistic? Or do most people prefer sin? Do most people prefer to live in the bad neighborhood?

While giving retreats at another beautiful sounding place (Tobyhanna, Pennsylvania) one year, I asked every group how they saw the world. Was it more evil or more good? The way I asked the question was to use the image of wheat or weeds in a field. The world is a field. Do you think it has more good or evil, more wheat or weeds?

I drew a line across a big piece of paper. On the left I put the word "wheat" and on the right I put "weeds." In the middle I put the number 50 and then went toward 100 on both sides, like this:

Wheat _____ Weeds

100　90　80　70　60　50　60　70　80　90　100

Then I asked each person to call out whether they thought the world was more wheat or weeds and then give a percentage. If you said 80 percent wheat then you were saying it's 20 percent weeds or vice versa. As each person called out I put a mark on the line. Most weekends we had about 55 men, so I had a visible sign what people were thinking at that moment. The majority thought there were more weeds than wheat, more evil than good in the world.

That didn't impress me as much as the striking contrasts that were exhibited in a group. Some people would think it was 90 percent weeds and three persons after that would say 90 percent wheat. Where does the truth lay? Is it a question of whether one is an optimist or a pessimist, whether one says the glass is half empty or half full? Or is the world more good than evil or vice versa. What do you think? Bring up the question the next time you are looking for something to talk about.

And what did I think? Every weekend after the group voted, I would say that I thought it was 90 percent wheat. The other priest I worked with would put it at around 70 percent weeds.

And looking at your own life? On a scale of 0-100, what's growing—more wheat or more weeds? Which side of the Golden Bridge are you living on? Which side do you prefer to live on?

Jesus came over the Golden Bridge as the new Moses to lead

us to the Promised Land. "To his own he came, yet his own did not accept him. Any who did accept him he empowered to become children of God" (John 1:11-12). He was killed, especially by those who thought they were on the right side, and didn't know they weren't.

"Father forgive them for they don't know what they are doing."

MANTRA: *"Remember the Golden Bridge."*

PART TWO
Helps in the Conversion Process

"I am the light of the world.
No follower of mine shall ever
walk in darkness, no they shall
possess the light of life."

(John 8:12)

11. TWO QUESTIONS

LAST year, when I was in Wisconsin, I had a great priest for a spiritual director—a Jesuit named Jim. At the end of a directed retreat at Wernersville, Pa., I asked my retreat director if he knew of any good spiritual directors in Wisconsin. Within two hours he gave me the name of two Jesuits at Marquette. Now that's networking. I wrote to one of them and asked if I could see him when I got to Wiscconsin.

Among other things, Jim gave me two good questions to begin a prayer period with:

1. What do I want from this period of prayer?
2. What does God want of me from this period of prayer?

Good questions help me to focus on issues. The two questions that Jim gave were very practical, so I began using them for beginning each day:

1. What do I want from this day?
2. What does God want of me this day?

And when I feel philosophical, I apply these two questions to my life:

1. What do I want from life?
2. What does God want for me in this life?

The first question is usually the easy one. I can come up with what I hope for in an hour of prayer, or during that day, or even for my life.

But it's in that second question that I am led into mystery. I've heard many answers to the question, "What is God's will?" However, I don't like the way people flip answers out and statements around concerning what is God's will.

Jesus sweated over "what is God's will," especially in the desert and in the garden. Then his followers come along and dribble out the quick comment, "It's God's will." And I find myself rattling back, "Is it?"

What is God's will? Can I ever really know it? The first Commandment warns against making false idols of God. A statue isn't God. Can our words ever be a true statement of God's words? Does God ever use words other than the word "Jesus"? All I can do is be quiet, and be in the presence of God and listen.

Now answers do come. Some, I'm sure, are autosuggestions from my imagination; hopefully, some are from God. For example, when I sit down to make a holy hour, I find myself answering the first question about what I want from this hour of prayer like this: "To be with you Lord"; or "To praise and thank you, Lord"; "To connect with you, Lord." But when I come to the second question I often hear suggestions like: "Shut up and listen"; or "Be still and be"; or "Be still and know that I am your God." At other times, I simply hear God answering, "To be with you, Andrew." And at other times, I feel blank and empty and keep looking at my watch.

1. What do I want?
2. What does God want for me?

When I came to this second section of this book, I found myself asking those questions again:

1. What do I want for this section of this book?
2. What does God want for this section?

Once again, the first question is relatively easy. I just presented the opening teaching of Jesus the Rabbi: that he is calling all of us to repentence, conversion, change, to a new life. Here in the second section, I'd like to provide some basic helps for the conversion process. I'd like to cover topics like private prayer, good reading, getting a spiritual director, finding a faith group, making a retreat, etc.

But "What does God want for this second section?"

Just to ask the question out loud sounds ridiculous. With all the questions we have about the Bible for someone writing a private book to claim a revelation of God's will would smack of stupidity and unbalance. Lock him up!

Yet, if I ask that question each day about what does God want of me this day, or in this hour of prayer, can't I ask the question of this section of this book? If I ask the Lord while I prepare a sermon, "What do you want me to say to your people, Lord," why can't I ask the question about what should I write in this book?

I don't know. I begin that way and then I add, based on the sayings of Jesus the Rabbi, that I would stress doing what Jesus did, and listening to what Jesus suggested. I would stress reading the prophets and spending hours in prayer with the Father. I would suggest helping your neighbor and helping the poor.

Then I would try to read the signs of the times, and be as practical as I possibly can, knowing that Jesus did not keep a journal, nor suggest that people use a rosary.

Now what?

Well, I leave you to try those two questions in your life or prayer or whatever this week—two questions I heard from an excellent Jesuit priest in Milwaukee.

MANTRA: *What do I want from this* _____?
          What does God want of me from this _____?
          (You fill in the blanks.)

12. READING THE PROPHETS

ONE of the most impressive persons I never met was the Jewish writer and theologian, Abraham Joshua Heschel. Now there was a rabbi.

Shortly before his death in 1972, NBC Television taped "A Conversation with Abraham Joshua Heschel" for its Eternal Light program. I hope they repeat that program from time to time because it does provide great light.

I can still hear Abraham Heschel saying how his life changed when he began reading and writing about the prophets. Before then, he said, he preferred staying in his study, writing, reading and learning. The prophets drove him out of his study and into the street. They forced him to get involved. He marched in the Civil Rights protests in the 60's and was one of the first to be against the war in Vietnam. He said that one of the saddest things in American contemporary life was that the prophets were unknown. Many intellectuals, who are great authorities on literature, he remarked, had never read the prophets, nor have they been touched by them.

Can we then say that many people who read and know the Gospels don't realize how much Jesus read and was touched, like Heschel was, by the prophets? Is that what pushed Jesus out of the carpenter shop and into the marketplace?

In his inaugural address in the synagogue in Nazareth, Jesus was handed the scroll of the prophet Isaiah. He unrolled the scroll and found the passage where Isaiah, the prophet, said:

> "The spirit of the Lord is upon me;
>   therefore he has anointed me.
> He has sent me to bring good news
>   to the poor,
>   to proclaim freedom to captives,
>   recovery of sight to the blind
>   and release to prisoners,
> to announce a year of favor from
>   the Lord."

51

Jesus rolled up the scroll. All were looking at him, wondering what their carpenter, now rabbi, was going to say. Pointing to the scroll, slowly carving out his words, Jesus said, "Today this scripture is fulfilled in your hearing" (Luke 4:14-30). Each of us needs to have Jesus point to us. Each of us needs to let Jesus carve us into the image we are called to be. Each of us needs to say in prayer, "Jesus, I am poor; give me good news. I am captive; free me. I am blind; give me sight. I am a prisoner; buy my release. Come, Lord Jesus. Walk into this temple, this synagogue called me, and fulfill those words of Isaiah in my hearing. Make this year a year of favor from the Lord."

If you want some challenging reading, start reading the prophets. Try the major prophets (Isaiah, Jeremiah and Ezechiel). If they hit home, next try the twelve minor prophets (Amos, Hosea, Michah, Zephaniah, Nahum, Habbakkuk, Haggai, Zechariah, Malachi, Obadiah, Joel and Jonah). A practical suggestion would be to start with the major prophets by reading the following chapters: Isaiah—Chapters 40, 55, 58, 61 and 65; Jeremiah—Chapters 5, 17, and 31; Ezechiel—Chapters 16, 34, and 37.

If you want to read an excellent book on the prophets, read *The Prophets* by Abraham Joshua Heschel. Listen to how he begins his book: "This book is about some of the most disturbing people who have ever lived; the men whose inspiration brought the Bible into being—the men whose image is our refuge in distress, and whose voice and vision sustain our faith." Many book stores sell *The Prophets* in a paperback, two volume set. Or check the library; they should have either the paperback edition or the one volume hardback issue, both from Harper and Row. As you read it, you'll find out why Heschel was challenged to get out of his study and into the mainstream of life.

The prophets challenge us to see what's really going on around us. They call us to conversion and change—to make decisions and to be more responsible with our gifts and talents. They challenge us to see beyond our nose and see our neighbor, especially those in distress or being abused. They see a lot more weeds than wheat.

The spirit (*Ruah* in Hebrew) sweeps over the waters and the prophet calls out, "Let there be light."

Don't we all need more light: to see who the poor, the captives, the blind, who the prisoners really are? Don't we all need more light: to see where we need more passion, compassion, and love in our lives?

MANTRA QUESTION: *How and when and where was the last time I was deeply challenged?*

13. READING THE BIBLE

AS I mentioned in an earlier meditation, St. Augustine tells us in his *Confessions* about how he heard a voice, probably that of a child, singing, "Take and read. Take and read!" It was in the midst of a great inner storm. He wasn't sure if he really could change his patterns. He couldn't overcome his sins, especially his sexual ones, and he kept putting off his conversion.

"Take and read. Take and read!"

He stopped for a minute, wondering where the voice was coming from. He figured out that it was a child in a nearby garden. Then he remembered the story of St. Anthony of Egypt who just happened to walk into a church as the Gospel was being read, "Go sell what you have and give to the poor and then come and follow me."

Anthony did as directed. So Augustine also did as directed and read a copy of Paul's letter to the Romans. His eyes fell upon the thirteenth chapter and those words were the grace he needed.

"Take and read. Take and read!"

We have to be ready. We have to keep asking those two questions.

1. What do I want from this moment of reading the Bible?
2. What does God want of me?

Before we open up the Bible we have to keep praying the prayer of Samuel in the temple, "Speak, Lord, for your servant is listening" (1 Samuel 3:9). Then we have to listen as we read, and as we pray.

In the seminary, in my first scripture course, we had Peter Ellis, writer, teacher, and lecturer. He was the most organized teacher I ever had. He got us to "take up and read" the scriptures. Each class lecture was outlined on the board as we walked into the class-

54

room. His book, *The Men and the Message of the Old Testament,*
is still an excellent text. However, the thing I remembered most
from Peter was a simple statement he once made: "Ninety percent of the Bible is clear; it's that other ten percent that causes
all the problems."

Then he said to forget about the ten percent and start reading
the Bible for the ninety percent. Simply read and reflect on the
different passages that are clear to you. Start with the prophets.
If they don't hit you, turn the pages. "Let your fingers do the
walking" to another section that you do understand.

We spend our energies and make our excuses for not reading
the Bible over the ten percent. We use the ten percent to divide
ourselves from other Christian groups.

"Take and read. Take and read."

Where should I begin? As suggested, begin with the prophets,
for example, one of the chapters that I mentioned in the last meditation. Or begin with the letter of James. I call James the "hard
hat" letter. I've yet to meet in person someone who doesn't understand and buy what James is saying. However, once again, people in the past argued about the ten percent and missed ninety
percent of James. The ten percent is the crazy argument about
faith and works. Something else was going on inside the Church
and outside the Bible in that argument. It could not have been James
2:14-20. If you don't understand what I'm talking about get a copy
of James and read it for yourself.

A great image and picture of how to read the Bible can be found
in the book of the prophet Ezechiel. In Chapters 2 and 3, Ezechiel
is told to eat a scroll that contained the word of God: " 'Son of
man, feed your belly and fill your stomach with the scroll I am
giving you!' I ate it. It was as sweet as honey in my mouth. 'Son
of man, go now to the house of Israel and speak my word to
them.' "

"Take and eat! Take and eat."

What a simple and what a profound way of reading the Bible.

Eat it. Digest it. However, to avoid indigestion cut it up first. Don't pig out on it, otherwise you'll burn out quickly on the Bible. Take a book at a time, or better, take a section at a time. Don't see the Bible as one book that you start from page one and go to the end. No, see it as a tableful of scrolls. See it as a library. Nobody goes into a library and starts reading the first book on the left or on the right. Too many people start with Genesis and get sick with indigestion with all those strange stories and names, the begets and begots, the people living for hundreds and hundreds of years. And if they are a more stubborn reader than most and they get through Genesis and Exodus, they bottom out with all the rules and regulations, laws and practices that are totally foreign to them in Leviticus and Numbers! It just isn't their type of food.

The Bible is a smorgasbord meal. Read what you like. Eat what's familiar to you. In time, you can try more exotic foreign foods. For example, begin with psalms, proverbs, and parables that you already know and like. Chew on them. Make them your own. And little by little the Bible is yours.

MANTRA: *"Take and read. Take and read."*

14. THE BIG BOOK

IN describing her experiences learning Buddhism and meditation in Thailand, Jane Hamilton-Merritt mentions that a wise old abbot in a wat in Bangkok used to tell her all the time, "One's self is the big book."

That made great sense to me because of an experience I had years ago. I got a phone call asking if I'd give a Sisters' retreat the following summer—eleven months away. I agreed and marked the date on my calendar. Four days later, the Sister who had called, wrote and asked what the theme of the retreat would be. I usually don't know what I'm going to do tomorrow. Here someone wanted to know what I was going to do eleven months later. On my desk was an autobiography that I was reading, so I wrote back that the theme would be "Autobiography."

Well, ten months and three weeks later, I was getting ready for that retreat, and I said to myself, "Autobiography? What the heck is that all about? What am I going to say about autobiographies for eight days?" I quickly went to my bookshelf and to any place where there were books in our house and got every book that looked anything like an autobiography. I put them in a few boxes and drove to the place I was to give the retreat.

Well, it was a nice accidental discovery for me. I hope the retreat helped the Sisters. It sure helped me. I discovered that people are fascinated by autobiographies. People are interested in people. On top of that, I discovered the idea of putting together one's own story. Write an autobiography.

"One's self is the big book."

Years later I attended a great workshop presented by Thomas Berry, during which he gave us a new creation account for the world we live in. For three days this brilliant Passionist priest gave the autobiography of our planet and its place in the solar system.

And he added that we are all called to read this revelation. In

fact, if I heard him right, there are four revelations that we need
to read:

1. Our story, that is the story, the revelation found in our own
life. This is the primary revelation.
2. Creation comes next. We need to study the revelation found
in creation—all that surrounds us: birds, rocks, trees, the sky,
change, etc.
3. History comes next. Not only do we need to study our own
history and the history of creation, we also need to study the story
of what has happened on the planet—especially how people have
lived and died, how people have treated people, etc. We need to
read history, the signs of the times, *The New York Times* and the
evening news.
4. And lastly, we need to read the scriptures of the world which
include the first three revelations.

Our story is primary. Our roots, our parents, our background,
the events and experiences of our own life, must be read. Everything has affected and formed us.
"Take and read. Take and read."
That made sense to me, because I had told the Sisters on that
retreat that I gave on "autobiography" to jot down all the facts
of their life: earliest memories, where they were born, where they
moved, significant moments, all the data they could jot down on
a time line. Next I told them to write down chapters, and then
begin writing in that framework.
A while later I attended Ira Progoff's "Intensive Journal Workshop." There it was again. The workshop had sessions where we
jotted down the significant stepping stones of our life. And during that journal workshop I got in touch with my childhood, remembering and jotting down events that were all but forgotten.
Along came the book and the movie *Roots*. Along came the
theology of story. Along came a lot of new books on journal keep-

ing. It was all coming together, this need to get in touch with the story of my life, chapter and verse.

Part of the conversion process would be to get in touch with blocks in one's life—along with the hidden joys, treasure and trash again. Some people spend years in therapy to get in touch with their past. Ordinarily, writing one's autobiography can be a great way to clarify the story of one's life. "Try it, you'll like it." It's good therapy.

The following are further practical suggestions.

1. Get a shoe box and gather all the photographs and slides and eight and super-eight MM. home movies that you can find of your childhood and youth. When you get a chance, look at these and jot down feelings and memories that hit you.

2. Next, do a time line of your life. If you have never seen it done, it can go as follows. Get a blank piece of paper and draw a line horizontally across the middle of the page. On the far left put the date of your birth. On the far right, put today's date. Then divide the line evenly and clearly in ten year periods. The next step is up to you. You can put in the most significant moments of your life first—jotting down a word like "marriage" and then draw a line down to the time line, so you can have plenty of room. If you run out of room, simply use another piece of paper. Or you can start at today's date and work backward to your birth date, marking down significant events.

3. Next, talk to your mom and dad, brothers and sisters, aunts and uncles, grandparents, whoever is living and knows about your family's roots. Use a tape recorder. Interview them with questions like, "What was I like as a baby?" "How did you feel when you were pregnant with me?" "What was it like?"

4. Next, write an outline of possible chapters for your autobiography or memoirs. Then start writing it, not for publication but for yourself.

5. Go to the library and check out other people's autobiographies. To grow in the spiritual life it would be well worth it to read auto-

biographies such as *The Confesssions* of St. Augustine, or the *Seven Storey Mountain* of Thomas Merton, or *The Story of a Soul*, the life of Therese Martin. Then there are excellent autobiographies like *Report to Greco* by Nikos Kazantzakis, or *The Long Loneliness* by Dorothy Day.

When we get our story together, we will find other people's stories more interesting and more connected to ours. We will become better listeners and more aware of other people's presence. We will discover what that abbot in Thailand meant when he said, "One's self is the big book."

MANTRA: *"One's self is the big book."*

15. SPIRITUAL DIRECTION

SPIRITUAL people, books, tapes keep suggesting, "Get a spiritual director."

And we answer back, "Who?"

Who and where are these holy men and women who will direct us in our prayer and in our spiritual life?

Thank God, some have appeared in the past 25 years. Not many, but some are around.

In my first 15 years as a priest, this was the one area where I had the greatest feelings of being a dummy. I didn't feel stupid for being ignorant about housing, school boards and zoning. But I felt like zero when a lady asked me to be her spiritual director. We had been trained that a priest was to be all things to all and to always be available. Then the lady asked me about John of the Cross. I didn't even know myself at the time.

That was a humbling experience and I went it alone. In those days hardly anyone had a spiritual director. Few priests even have one today. Confessors, yes, spiritual directors, no. So after a while I had to admit to myself and the lady that I was not a spiritual director.

What helped make me conscious was a course in spiritual direction that I began to take. A friend of mine, Frank, told me about a two year course being offered by two Capuchin priests, Benedict Groeschel and Regis Armstrong, at the diocesan seminary in New York. It consisted of three lectures, one morning a week. Here was a good opportunity for me to take a day off a week, see Frank, a priest at S. Cecilia's in Spanish Harlem, hear three talks, and play some basketball in the afternoon. Benedict Groeschel, psychologist, gave two talks: one on counseling and one on spiritual direction. Regis Armstrong, historian, gave the other lecture, taking us through the history of Christian spirituality.

It was and still is the dream of Benedict to develop a pool of spiritual guides and directors for the New York area. He had discovered that so many people had left the religious life and priesthood without ever talking to anyone, except perhaps, if they had fallen in love, with the person they were in love with. Then when they applied for dispensation papers, they were advised by their bishops or supervisors to talk to Benedict or some counselor or director. And Benedict found out the obvious truth; it was too late. The horse was out of the barn. Their minds were already made up. They didn't want direction, they wanted their papers.

So Benedict's goal was to get people talking to spiritual directors all through their life and not just in time of trouble and crises.

Times have changed. Things have improved. Many Sisters and Brothers and Priests who had training in psychology during the seventies, began to see how important that step was in their life. Often they thought it was to help others, only to find out they were doing it for themselves. They gained the most. Then they began to see they needed the next step, integrating psychology with spirituality.

Today, these are some of the people who are leading the way in what Edward Sellner, Henri Nouwen, Martin Thornton, and others call our most important, if not our greatest pastoral need—being spiritual directors. Compare 1960 seminary catalogues with the catalogues of today. Take a look at the programs and workshops offered by most dioceses. Check out how many women have entered the field of spiritual direction and counseling.

It's become very clear that priests are not automatically qualified to be spiritual directors by reason of their ordination. At times church authorities seem to think that. As Thomas Merton pointed out in his classic book on *Spiritual Direction and Meditation,* in the early Church in the Egyptian and Syrian deserts it was personal holiness and not the priesthood that gave spiritual directors their role.

People looking for a deeper spiritual life are looking for guides and directors who have done their homework. They are looking for men and women who have taken courses and made workshops in counseling and in spiritual direction. They are looking for people who have made directed retreats, read the books and articles, listened to the tapes, have had supervision, did their verbatims, made their mistakes and have learned from them. They are looking for people who make their holy hours, have a director themselves, and are growing in the spiritual life.

Unfortunately, many priests don't qualify. They don't even qualify as good confessors. And then the lay people are blamed for not going to confession. The renewal of the Church is going to bypass all those who are not willing to be renewed themselves.

If there is any one message that hit me in Merton's book on *Spiritual Direction and Meditation* it's the message of equating magic with the spiritual. Spiritual direction is not magic. The spiritual director is not a magician. Spiritual growth is hard work and it calls for dying. It calls for generosity. It calls for honesty. It calls for dialogue. I would suspect that Merton would have destroyed anyone who came to him to get bragging rights that he had a spiritual director and it was Thomas Merton.

I would also add that the magical and automatic has to go in several other areas. So many priests think that sermons, "saying Mass," hearing confessions, visiting the sick, all work automatically, just by doing them. And the numbers keep going down. Meanwhile, the faithful who remain wish their parishes would publish who says what mass so they could choose the best Mass to go to and which Masses to avoid.

Now, of course, that thought is heresy to some priests, especially those who are not in touch with people. But where is there a Catholic who doesn't say things like, "Every time our associate pastor walks down the aisle for Mass I say, 'Oh no, not again!'" Or, "St. John's has the best Mass in the area."

Homilies, the liturgy, confession, baptisms, visiting the sick, like spiritual direction, are all person to person experiences and when they are made I-IT experiences, people who want an I-THOU experience go "Yuck!" Read Martin Buber's classic book, *I-Thou* and you can hear all this in more professional terms.

I write all this not just to air my gripes, but because of my love for the Church. I hope more and more Sisters, Brothers, Lay People, become spiritual directors, but I also want to see priests take up this calling. Then their own spiritual life will be exposed like mine was. They will see the need for help, for spiritual direction, etc. Then, hopefully, their new life will flow into their homilies, the Sacrament of Reconciliation, and the prayers of the liturgy will be prayers and not just words, words, words.

The reason for the shortage of priests can be found here, as well as the solution. We don't need gimmicks or slick promotion or young dynamic vocation directors. We need people—people, who are spiritual role models.

Having aired all that, let's return to our opening question about who and where are these spiritual directors for someone who wants a deeper spiritual life.

The first step is to ask around. Ask, "Who's a good spiritual director?" When you get a few names, check them out. Don't we do that when seeking doctors and dentists and chiropractors?

Next, contact the person you hope for and express your need. The best spiritual directors will probably be tied up in a busy schedule. If she says "no," then that's a good sign. You would want someone who could say "no." Then ask them if there is anybody they would recommend.

Once you get someone, make a deal to be with them for about five sessions, once a month, for five months. At that point make a mutual evaluation of how things are going and then give yourself and the director the option of continuing or ending the relationship. This needs to be mentioned up front right from the beginning. Not everybody is everybody's cup of tea.

What should you be aware of in those first five sessions? Look for someone with experience, experience, experience. Look for someone with training in spiritual direction, someone who can listen, gives good advice, good common sense, and can see where you are. Look for someone who challenges you, getting at your patterns, your quirks, and your needs. Warning signals should go off in your brain if the director has no guidelines, no time limits, and begins using you to figure out his or her story. Listen to your gut, as they say in counseling.

However, if someone seems green and new at spiritual direction you might want to give them a chance if you sense great possibilities. Everybody has to start somewhere. Listen to your heart. Can you trust this person? Does the person seem prudent? Do they pray with you at the beginning, during, and at the end of the session? Is it natural and comfortable?

And check around and locate several good books and magazine articles about spiritual direction, spiritual guides, soul friends, spiritual friends, etc. They will help you in your search.

QUOTE: *"A penny for your thoughts."*

—Swift

16. LEARNING HOW TO FOCUS

I WOULD think the first issue in spiritual direction is the issue of focusing. In biblical terms it's the question God asked Adam and Eve in the garden, "Where are you?"

They were hiding in the bushes. They had eaten of the tree of the knowledge of good and evil. Now they knew the possibility of choice. Now they knew the possibility of evil besides good. Now they knew they were naked. They would never be the same again. They had come of age.

Where are you? What happened to Adam and Eve happens to everyone—unless that person never grows up. Some people don't discover this amazing responsibility, this amazing gift, this amazing freedom, that they have. We can choose the wrong thing. We are responsible for our actions.

Have you ever focused in on that reality? Where are you on this question of freedom and responsibility?

Most people don't realize it till they make a mistake and discover their nakedness and hide their face in shame. Till some marriages fall apart, they are a drifting existence. I remember reading a book review in which a boy in a Texas town was described as never having a thought above his belt buckle. I heard someone describe a woman in her 20's, "Oh, she thinks with her crotch." What happens if both get married to each other? Time will tell.

Some people don't think. They float. The result is a time bomb that leads to an explosion and chaos.

Where are you?

Where are you in your relationships? What's going on in your life right now? What is the quality of your life? Do you pray?

I remember listening to a tape by Sidney Simon, who is famous for his *Value Clarifications* processes. He said he asks young people questions such as where would they like to be on a Saturday, if they had a choice: a) the beach, b) the woods, or c) a shopping mall. And most, he said, raised their hands for either the beach or the woods. Then he would ask where they spent their last five Saturdays.

We vote with our feet, not our mouth. We vote with the way we use our time, not our promises.

When we go to a doctor, we get weighed and poked and examined. We are asked questions. The doctor focuses in on our health, where we are, what's going on in our body. We are also given tests. Blood and urine can often tell more than our words.

A good spiritual director should help us to see where we are. After the small talk and the ice breaking, after the trust level is built up, we should begin to see the wheat and the weeds in our field. We should know that most people begin spiritual direction hiding in the bushes. The purpose is not to down us, but to lift us. St. Ignatius in his exercises, says that "the one who is giving the exercise should not seek to investigate and know the private thoughts and sins of the person making the exercise. Nevertheless, it will be very helpful if he is kept faithfully informed about the various disturbances and thoughts caused by the action of different spirits. This will enable him to propose some spiritual exercises in accordance with the degree of progress made and suited and adapted to the needs of a soul disturbed in this way" (Introductory Observation #17).

Discernment of spirits, focusing of energies, clarification of values, seeing our real priorities: these are the early tasks of spiritual direction.

Or as Jesus the Rabbi put it, "Where your treasure is, there also is your heart."

Focusing

Focus...learning how to focus...learning how to clarify ...learning how to target, instead of being all over the place... learning how to discern where to begin.

Will the new fully automatic cameras prevent people from learning how to focus?

At slide shows or home movies and even in movie theaters we all have had the experience of someone or maybe the whole crowd yelling out in frustration: "FOCUS!"

Imagine if the whole crowd in church on Sunday yelled out at the preacher: "FOCUS!"

In the seminary, when we were taught how to put sermons together, we not only had to hand in a complete sermon, but we also had to present the sermon in one sentence. And that one sentence had to have more than the subject we would be speaking on. It had to state what we were predicating about the subject.

It took time and energy. Clear thinking is like that. But it taught us how to focus. Maybe the preacher should be forced to put the subject of his sermon and what he or she is predicating about it in the parish bulletin in one clear sentence.

David Belasco, a theatrical producer, used to say, "If you can't write your idea on the back of my calling card, you don't have a clear idea."

Well, that's what we do in spiritual direction. However, it takes time. Spiritual direction is not a grueling cross-examination in police station style, but to make a pun, it is a cross examination. We need to focus on where the cross and dying itself needs to take place.

Possible areas: relationships, self-esteem, prayer, work, vocation, ministry, anger, recreation, laziness, sexuality, lack of energy, slowing down, getting older, death, temptations, weight, neglects, how I spend my Sundays, community life, family, marriage, discipline, fasting, use of time, structures, reading, work.

If disturbances come up in which the person under spiritual direction needs counseling or other help, the spiritual director needs to discern this. In our age, lawsuits or their possibility force people who offer themselves as spiritual directors to focus on being responsible, to know what they are doing, and what the role of a spiritual director is and is not.

Deciding Which Battles to Fight

The benefit then of spiritual direction is the clarification, the centering in, the focusing on where we are.

Then comes the work. Labeling problems or issues doesn't settle them. However, it's often a relief to know what's going on, what's disturbing us. The director then, as Ignatius points out, suggests exercises that will help the person being directed.

Here's where a wise director comes in. A good rule to follow is to pick your battles. Don't start with the most difficult ones. Keep some problems on the shelf. Learning how to retreat is a strategy. Pick battles where you'll see results. Pick battles that are visible and manageable. Pick ones that get to the root of things. Pick ones that are nagging us and make us feel small and slow because we're not dealing with them.

MANTRA: *"Where are you?"*

17. LEARNING HOW TO PRAY

IN *Sentimental Journey,* James Barrie wrote that the commonest prayer in all languages is, "Oh God, if I were sure I were to die tonight I would repent at once."

In the meanwhile many of us don't pray until the next tragedy hits us. And then we say, "Oh God, no!" or "Jesus Christ!" or "Holy Cow!" Listen to people's spontaneous remarks when they see an accident or a near car crash in person or on television. There is usually some type of spontaneous prayer or cry for help.

Then there are two other types of people: those who pray all their lives and are satisfied with the way they are praying and those who pray but want to learn to pray better.

One of the main reasons people go to spiritual directors is to learn how to pray. If there is any one question I have heard asked the most by people over 40 on retreats it has been the question "Can you give me any suggestions on how to pray?"

Times don't change on that one. The disciples often saw Jesus praying, and so they asked, "Lord, teach us how to pray." Then Jesus the Rabbi taught his disciples two things about prayer. First he gave them the Our Father prayer. And then he gave them two parables about our Father. The first parable says to keep nagging God, asking, seeking, knocking on his door. The second parable says that God is a father who will give us what we need. "What father among you will give his child a snake if he asks for a fish or hand him a scorpion if he asks for an egg" (Luke 11:1-13).

How should I pray? Start with the Our Father. We all know it by heart—which sometimes means by rote rather than by heart. Try it. Say it slowly. Chew each part. Digest it. Make it your own.

One of the best night prayers that I have come up with is this: Before going to bed, find a quiet place where you can be alone. Married people could do this together. Pause. Stretch out your arms in prayer like Jesus on the cross. Then think of the nicest moment of that day. Choose one moment—the best thing that happened to you that day. Then pause and realize that there are other people right that very moment praying, saying the Our Father. Then pray it out loud slowly with them in a deep prayer of gratitude and petition. That's it! It takes no more than two or three minutes.

So Jesus' first teaching about prayer when asked how to pray was to give his disciples a formula or set prayer. And isn't that the way we all begin to learn how to pray? We heard formulas at home and at church. We learned by rote the prayers of our childhood.

Unfortunately, some people never get beyond that. Now when it comes to prayer, set prayers are not the problem. The problem is the person saying them: if he or she is simply babbling the words, being superstitious, mechanical or childish, or just being blah, then it's time for a change of attitude and perhaps a change of prayers.

All religions have set prayer formulas. Some are junk prayers and some are good prayers. It would be better to say three good prayers than twenty-three junk prayers. Some people get all kinds of prayers enclosed in mailing pieces looking for money for seminarians or the missions and are unable to throw them out. Then they put them into a prayerbook that ends up having more prayer cards than pages. As my sister Peggy would say, "Pitch!" Pitch out the junk.

Where are you? A director needs to help a person see where they are in their relationship with God. To focus on this, questions need to be asked about how the person prays. Thomas Merton points out in his book on *Spiritual Direction and Meditation* that the issue here is not degrees of prayer, or where a person is on the mountain of prayer, or whether a person has infused or acquired contemplation. The question is not whether a person takes his or her prayer seriously, but whether they take God seriously.

Dom Chapman said, "Pray as you can and don't try to pray as you can't." That's a good rule to keep in mind when you are getting confused or bogged down in prayer. It's especially true and we don't even need the rule when there is a tragedy. We start praying as we can when our brother is dying of cancer. It's like the comment we make about people who speak several languages fluently, "I wonder what language they pray in." If they say prayers in several languages, then I wonder what language they pray in when they are in a car accident or a loved one is seriously sick.

People interested in prayer should go to God first, not to a book. Ask God, seek God, and keep knocking on God's door. "Lord, teach me how to pray."

Next, people who do or don't have a spiritual director should read or listen to a few of the excellent books, articles or tapes that are around on prayer. Ask a religious Sister for a recommendation for a good book on prayer. Ask your local priest. Ask spiritual directors. Archbishop Anthony Bloom's excellent book, *Beginning to Pray* (Paulist Press) is out in a new edition. Anthony De Mello, S.J. has several books out on spiritual exercises that are very helpful for prayer. *The National Catholic Reporter* publishes a supplement, magazine size, called *Praying,* four times a year. In it you'll find suggestions for tapes and lots of other resources for prayer. It's all there if you want it.

St. Alphonsus, who started the community of religious that I belong to, the Redemptorists, got an honorary doctorate from the Church for his teachings about prayer. Being practical and someone who borrowed the best from everyone, he came up with a simple formula for what he called "mental prayer" as opposed to vocal prayer. It has three basic steps: 1) THE PREPARATION, 2) THE MEDITATION, and 3) THE CONCLUSION. It goes as follows:

1. *THE PREPARATION:* Line up for yourself a set amount of time for prayer, for example, a half hour. Find a good place where you can pray. Try to get your business out of the way so you will have fewer distractions during your prayer. Take a body position that is suitable for prayer. Use some set prayers or pray in your own words for help during your time of prayer.

2. *THE MEDITATION:* This is the main part of "mental prayer." Use a book to get some thoughts. Stop whenever something hits you. Alphonsus said "St. Teresa of Avila used a book for 17 years; she would read a little, then meditate for a short time on what she read. It is useful to meditate in this way, in imitation of the pigeon that first drinks and then raises its eyes to heaven."

Next come prayers. This is why one reads. The main advantage of your reading and reflections is that you should be led to a) affections, b) petitions and c) resolutions.

a. *Affections:* For example, you're meditating on the Gospel story of Jesus deep in prayer in Luke (11:1-4) and the disciples seeing Jesus praying ask, "Lord, teach us how to pray." Feelings arise in you, and you begin praising God for the way he has been teaching you how to pray. Or you begin to express sorrow and sadness for your lack of prayer in spending so much time in watching television.

b. *Petitions:* Then you start asking Jesus to teach you how to pray. You become quiet and you hear him teach you the Our Father in a new way. Then you start praying it in the new way yourself, asking God for help in all the areas that you need help in.

c. *Resolutions:* Before you finish your set prayer time, St. Alphonsus advises that you make some promises and resolutions. It might be a practical resolution to take a day at a time, or to say the Our Father slowly that day at Mass, or to forgive a co-worker "who trespassed against you." Make it as specific and practical as possible. Name names. See situations you will be in.

3. *THE CONCLUSION:* Sum up your prayer period with a prayer of thanks for the graces and light you received during your period of prayer. Renew your promises and resolutions. Ask Mary, the woman in whom the word became flesh, to help you put your words into flesh, into practice. Pray for the sick, the most abandoned, sinners, the dead.

Most of the prayer formulas in the West go somewhat like that. The books all give some type of format. Take one and try it for a while. It might become you.

Or you can use centering prayer, using a mantra or the Jesus prayer, or other Eastern methods of prayer.

The point is not how to pray. We don't get wrapped up in how we communicate. We communicate. But every once and a while it's good to step back and see how we communicate, and maybe there are better ways.

MANTRA: *"Lord, teach us how to pray."*

18. JOURNAL WORK

ONE of the most practical techniques in spirituality that has re-emerged is that of keeping a journal. In fact, it has become so common that recently a person making a directed retreat told her retreat director, "I'll do anything but journal work. I'm sick of hearing about it."

If that's the case, back off. She had been to six workshops and three retreats in the past few years and everybody had pushed keeping a journal.

But what's the big deal? It's simply the old idea of keeping a diary or a journal of what's happening in one's life. My sister-in-law, Joanne, suggested that I keep a diary when I went to Italy a few years back. She had gone to Africa twice and she said it was the best souvenir from the trip. You pick it up a few years later and you are back in Africa, especially if you jotted down all kinds of interesting tidbits and observations.

Spiritual directors and therapists often suggest writing down dreams and significant events in one's life. People who need to lose weight are asked to jot down what they eat each day, the time, and also the mood they were in, plus experiences that might have affected one's moods. The obvious point would be learning if moods affect eating habits.

Edward Albee, the playwright, said that he writes to unclutter his mind. I don't know about you, but writing this book has been great for me. I usually write a meditation, then let it sit, then rewrite it over and over again, till I'm satisfied or till I say "enough; you'll never get this book finished."

Here is a list of words. Get a note book or scraps of paper and write about 750 words on each word. Do fifty-two words, and you'll have a book like this. Begin with the word and add "for me means" and go from there:

Loneliness	Mom	Love	Recognition
Happiness	Dad	Hate	Worship
Anger	Brother	Rejection	Sex
Pressure	Sister	Hurt	Peace
Recreation	Children	Forgiveness	Money

Or complete the following sentences, turning them into a 750 word essay.

> I hate it when...
> I love it when...
> I feel lonely when...
> I wish they would...
> I feel great when...
> I wonder what would happen if...
> I can't stand it when...

Or dream dreams for yourself and your world using the following topics:
> Work
> Family
> Marriage
> Children
> Church
> Hunger
> Old People
> The Arms Race

Or read next Sunday's readings and put together the sermon you would like to preach or you would want to hear.

Or as Sidney Simon urges, write a letter to the following people:

> Dear Pope,
> Dear Bishop,

Dear President,
Dear Mayor,
Dear Pastor,
Dear Boss,
Dear Newspaper,

Diary manufacturers, according to an article in the *New York Times Magazine*, estimated that more than five million blank books or empty diaries are sold each year. Now, not everyone uses those blank books or diaries. Often birthday or Christmas gifts soon get put aside, but those who keep a diary or jot down ideas find it a rather cheap form of therapy.

The choice is yours!

MANTRA: *"Make an account of your stewardship."*

19. SPIRITUAL READING

ONE priest I went to for spiritual direction had the knack of handing me the right book at the right time. He'd listen well, then go to his bookshelf and come back with a book: "Here try this." He always reminded me of the words of Jesus the Rabbi, "Every scribe who is learned in the reign of God is like the head of a household who can bring from his storeroom both the new and the old" (Matthew 13:52).

Where do these people get time to read? Great readers always amaze me, especially those who have quite busy schedules. A good spiritual director needs to know not only the classics, but also the modern books. She or he has to read the reviews and then read the best books and articles and listen to the tapes. They have to ask and scout around for the best.

We need to remember the old adage: "Beware of the person of one book." Yet, we also need to heed the warnings of Schopenhauer, Bacon and Hobbes, all of whom spoke against too much reading. By that they meant overdosing without stopping to think, question, compare and assimilate what we are reading. Bacon used the image of eating what you're reading, the same image the Ezechiel the prophet used, distinguishing between "books to be tasted, others to be swallowed, and some few to be chewed and digested."

So we have to read, but we can't rush it. We have to read, but we have to be careful of what we read. It becomes us. Tennyson, in his poem "Ulysses," says, "I am part of all that I have met." And another poet, George Seferis, said, "Don't ask who's influenced me. A lion is made up of the lambs he's digested, and I've been reading all my life."

What was the best book you read in the past year? Would you recommend it? Did it make you think, laugh, cry? Were there any changes in your life as a result? Did it overshadow your life, your work, everything, for the week or so that you were reading it? Did it move you in spiritual ways—help you to pray better?

The number of spiritual books that have appeared in the past two decades has been amazing. Anybody who has been going to the Newman Book Store in Washington, D.C. over the past 15 years has seen the spiritual reading section gobble up more and more room, more and more shelf space.

Somebody's reading those books.

Then there are the novels. Greg, a novice I had in Wisconsin, kept on telling me to read Flannery O'Connor. Joe, a college student in Philadephia, sent me three novels by Walker Percy. Joanne, my sister-in-law, keeps saying to me, "How can you be a priest and not read good novels?" My excuse was always that I didn't even have enough time to read the technical stuff. When am I going to get time to read the novels? Then it finally hit me, the novelists are talking about life and what's going on in people. Now I try to read five novels a year!

Where do you read? In the big building where I am living, this is not an issue. But "in the real world" this obviously is a problem for some people. First, there is the bathroom. That's the place for magazines and books like this that provide short meditations.

Then there's the garage. Yes, the garage. Al, a friend of mine, fixed up a small chapel in his garage. He escapes there to listen to tapes, to pray, and to read. He installed a heater, a kneeler, and a small spiritual library. He ought to rent it out to people looking for a quiet place to hide.

I once saw in *The New York Times* an interesting suggestion for a place to read or to pray. A woman named Pat Day discovered that you can get a private room in a bank, at least in New York City, at your disposal during the day for only $12 dollars a year.

She said all you need to do was rent a safe deposit box. Show up at the bank with your card. Ask for your box and a private room. A guard will take you to your room. You close the door. Free at last! The room has no windows, so it doesn't make any difference whether it's winter or summer, rainy or snowy, hot or cold. The room is at a set temperature.

It's perfect, she said, for a quiet place to eat your lunch and read a book.

I doubt that most banks would provide such a service, but once the book bug hits you, you'll be as ingenious as Pat Day and my friend Al were.

MANTRA: *Read any good books lately?*

20. I SHALL RETREAT

ONE of the best moves for growth and inner peace is to make a retreat. Fortunately, there are many retreat houses scattered all over the country. Most are in scenic places, near mountains, rivers, lakes, woods, the desert, the Atlantic, the Pacific, and the Gulf of Mexico.

Having spent 14 years working in two different retreat houses, I saw firsthand the obvious benefits of a retreat. The first is in the very word. It's an escape, a retreat from the business of life. The second benefit is also in the word. It's a time to re-treat the basics of life. You can see a lot more from the mountain than from the valley. Distance makes the heart see better.

By now most people are over the old complaint and fear that a retreat is a few days spent totally on your knees, "all prayer and no breaks." The highly structured and policed high school retreats of the thirties, forties and fifties gave a whole generation of people that impression about retreats.

The high school retreats of the sixties and the seventies were guitars, folk songs, slide shows, fun and games, fear of pot and six-packs, trying to quiet radios and stereos, crowded-around-the-altar liturgies, a 16 millimeter movie called "The Parable," pizza at 11 p.m. and several other serendipitous experiences.

The Marriage Encounter and Cursillo came along and got people active, busy, challenged and made to work for a whole weekend. Couples could not escape from each other on a Marriage Encounter weekend. They had to write a whole batch of letters to each other about money, kids, their relationship, their future, their sex life, their relatives, and anything and everything that was mulching around in their guts. The Cursillo, usually Thursday night till Sunday, gave Catholics a good mini-course in their faith. Both helped make the old, talked-at-type retreat even more out of touch. It forced the traditional weekend retreats to add discussion groups

81

and use more of a team approach. Some retreat houses added religious and lay people to their staff.

Have you ever made a retreat? What was it like? When was your last retreat? If you never made a retreat or haven't made one in a while, plan on one. It's one of the best moves you can make. Ask around and you'll find out where you can make one, the cost, and type of retreats offered.

Retreats help break patterns! Retreats help start patterns. Look at what happened to Jesus the Rabbi, after spending 40 days and 40 nights in the desert.

One of the best choices I made in the last few years was to make an eight day directed retreat at the Jesuit Spirituality Center at Wernersville, Pa. For me it was a teachable moment, a special time of grace, during which I approached Jesus in prayer, like a student listening to a great teacher.

Surprise! It was eight days of silence and eight days of prayers. And it was modern!

The location is absolutely beautiful, but that wasn't what hit me. In fact, I made my retreat with about 40 other people in cold, frozen January. What hit me was the one-to-one with Jesus and the one-to-one experience with a director. My director, Frank, another great Jesuit priest, simply gave me passages from the Bible that were fitted for what I was saying and feeling. Each day I was to make three holy hours on a passage or two from the Bible. After each holy hour, I was to break from prayer, walk around, and then jot down what came up during that hour of prayer. In my daily meeting with Frank, I would let him know from my jottings what was going on. That was it. There were no talks other than the daily homily at Mass.

A retreat. Try it, you'll like it.

As Teilhard de Chardin said, "The specific strength of a retreat lies in making God real again."

QUESTION: *Is there anything preventing me from making a retreat?*

21. A PRAYER COMMUNITY

BESIDES a spiritual director, spiritual reading, journal keeping, private prayers, and a good retreat, another help in the ongoing conversion process is finding a prayer community.

We are living in the age of support groups. Just check the local paper or the bulletin board at the supermarket and you'll see notices about support groups for people with cancer, people who have lost children, people with kids on drugs, people with children with all kinds of sicknesses, widows groups, post-mastectomy, post-lumpectomy support groups, Emotions Anonymous, Gamblers Anonymous, Overeaters Anonymous, Alcoholics Anonymous, Singles Again, Parents Without Partners, Quest, Focus, etc.

However, support groups have always been around. When things get rough, the marriage gets shaky, the kids are getting on the nerves, or one feels all alone, a lot of people head for the local bar, the Moose Lodge, the Knights of Columbus, the Ladies Auxiliary, or any of their equivalents.

Reports and studies point out at times that Catholics are often frustrated by big parishes. They feel anonymous that "nobody knows my name!" Renew, Genesis II, and a host of other programs have made a dent in solving this problem.

Where are the support groups for those who want to pray? The old novenas certainly helped. It was a chance to pray together for a while and then stop and talk in the back of the church or outside before heading home. It didn't have the rush or the crowds of Sunday Mass. One felt special. One felt connected to others.

One answer has been the charismatic prayer groups that are everywhere. In many places you'll find normal, everyday people who are trying to grow in their spiritual life. Sometimes people get put off by "praying in tongues" and "being slain in the spirit," but if the group puts the gifts of prayer and charity in the forefront and doesn't get bogged down by the extraordinary, then you might find a home there. Usually the music and the family atmosphere provide good support for those for whom this form of prayer is appealing. Moreover, time has separated from the groups those who might have joined because it was the latest fad in spirituality.

Another form of prayer support group is what is called a "Shared Prayer Group." The group consists of a small number—three, four, five or six people. "Where two or three are gathered together in my name, you'll find me there in the middle of the group."

Literature on how to set up such a group is around. Ask, seek, knock, and you'll find people and the means of starting or joining such a group. If you're interested in starting a "Shared Prayer Group," I would make the following suggestions:

1. Meet regularly—at least every week or every two weeks. Meet even if all cannot be there. Stability and regularity are very important.

2. Start at a set time and end at the set time. I would recommend an hour. In my opinion, groups die when people keep coming late or through never ending at the agreed on time, or by not having times agreed upon. Baby sitters and other members of the family are involved. People are more apt to continue in a group when they know the group does what it agreed upon. As the old saying goes, "People with nothing to do usually try to waste time with people who have something to do."

3. Come to pray, not to discuss. You have to clearly define the purpose of the group. It's prayer. If you want to establish an adult education group, or a faith sharing group, make sure you label and advertise it as such. However, the prayer group should name one of its meetings, say every two months, as an evaluation session on how the prayer group is doing. That's the time for gripes, suggestions, etc.

4. Pick a place that is free from interruptions, disturbances, distractions, and telephones.

5. Have lots of silence. Quiet down. Listen. Listen to each other's prayers. Don't piggyback. Listen to the scripture texts someone might be led to read. Listen to a song someone might play to create

an atmosphere. "Shared prayer" as someone said, "is silence interrupted by prayer, not prayer interrupted by silence."

6. Follow the two rules of a Quaker meeting:
   a) Don't come with the idea that you are going to say something.
   b) Don't come with the idea that you're not going to say something.

7. Pick someone as a leader who will begin the prayer and end the prayer. Rotate the leader, because clock watchers and leaders also need to be free of worries so they can be free to pray.

8. Having made those suggestions, it would be important to state the last rule. "Don't get caught up in rigidity with rules and regulations."

Can such a group last? I've run into groups that have been excellent prayer support groups and have lasted for years. I see the key ingredients to be that the group prays, and that the group meets regularly for a set period of time, and that the members be dedicated to prayer and the group.

I ran into a rosary group down in a big parish outside of Philadelphia. They meet every Monday night from 7 to 7:15. It's a no frills group. No cake, no coffee, just a bunch of people from different houses on this street who know there is a rosary every Monday night at a set time on that street.

MANTRA: *"Where two or three are gathered in my name, there I am in their midst" (Matthew 18:20)*.

22. ROSARY BEADS AREN'T JUST FOR HAIL MARY'S ANY MORE

MIKE, a novice from last years's class, brought a pair of worry beads back from Israel. He didn't say if they were a hint or what? I have heard of worry beads but I'm not sure just how you use them. Do you use them for prayers? Do you use them to count your worries?

Take the rosary that Catholics use. Most have a rosary in their hands when they are buried. Some have one in their hands when they are alive. Most have a pair somewhere in their bottom drawer or in a box in their cellar. They are both worry beads and prayer beads and many times those two needs run together.

Who said rosary beads are just for Hail Mary's? Why not use them for short Bible quotes, mantras, wisdom sayings, short prayers, etc.?

Mantra is a Sanskrit word for a mystical formula or prayer or incantation. The Hail Mary, with its two parts, is a bit long, but it works as a mantra and prayer formula. It seems better when it is broken in two, and two or more people say its parts. The same goes for the Our Father prayer.

The beauty of the rosary is that we know the words. The more we say them, the more they can fade into the background, allowing us to go deeper and deeper into prayer. The Hail Mary's give us space. The rosary in our hands tells us that we're in the space of prayer. It sets the mood for prayer. The Hail Mary's are background music, so we can become centered on where we are. I used to wonder why people worried and confessed having distractions while saying the rosary. The distractions are what it's all about. The distractions should be the prayers. Concentration on the words can sometimes destroy the whole purpose of the rosary: prayer.

However, when I read Jane Hamilton-Merritt's book, *A Meditator's Diary,* I noticed that in some meditation practices the trick is to concentrate on the formula, saying it over and over again, as in centering prayer. She describes the practice of counting to ten. Start breathing with one-in, one-out, two-in, two-out. When your mind wanders, gently bring it back and start concentrating with one-in, one-out, two-in, two-out again. Jane Hamilton-Merritt said how difficult it was to get beyond "two" in the beginning "without my mind rebelling from the task at hand." However, after a while, it became part of her and she moved down to some serious business in the center of her life.

When I was stationed at our retreat house at Tobyhanna, Pennsylvania, somebody long years ago had set up the practice of saying the rosary during the weekend retreats. At first I thought it was old fashioned and a bit too much, till I experienced the genius of it. After the orientation on Friday evening, after supper on Saturday evening, and after the final conference on Sunday, the whole gang of us on retreat would walk around the building saying the rosary. A different person would lead each decade. While doing that I realized it got us to shut up. It gave us time to digest ideas and food. And it also gave us time to do some deeper spiritual thinking. It was a mood setter for people to meditate on all kinds of issues, especially the joyful, the sorrowful and the glorious mysteries of life. Moreover, like seeds underground, we don't know what's happening underneath when we pray, but we make an act of faith that God the Creator will help things grow thirty, sixty and a hundred fold.

In our provincial headquarters in Brooklyn we had an old brother named Walter. I often saw him in chapel there saying a rosary. When he died, I was away, so I couldn't get to his funeral. Two weeks later, I noticed his rosary in his seat in chapel. Two days later it was there in the same spot, so I stole it. I used it for a while, praying for Walter and some prayers of gratitude for his example of prayer. It was in my pocket when I was visiting my brother. We were talking about God and prayer and sickness and death. I gave him Walter's rosary and told him it would help him pray when he had trouble sleeping and praying. I told him to use

it to repeat over and over again prayers like "Help!" or "Lord,
give Joanne and the girls strength. Give them courage."

I didn't realize until then that I had been using my rosary beads
while driving and while praying, to repeat short prayers and Bible sayings over and over again.

Up until the arrival from the East of the Jesus Prayer ("Lord
Jesus Christ, have mercy on me") and mantras, and worry beads,
some Catholics seemed to have been embarrassed by the rosary
and by repeating the same prayer over and over and over again.
Now that we understand these gifts from other cultures, we have
come full circle, as John S. Dunne of Notre Dame would put it,
and we'll begin to see the value of the rosary.

Check your bottom drawer or the boxes in the cellar and I'm
sure you'll find a rosary. When you die they'll just have to look
in your pocket or pocketbook and find your rosary for the
undertaker.

So my suggestion in this book is to use your rosary not only
for Hail Mary's, but also for the mantras, prayers, or quotes that
I give at the end of each meditation. Try saying those words a
couple of hundred times that week.

MANTRA: Use a rosary this week saying over and over again
on the beads these words from The Hail Mary:
"The Lord is with you."

PART THREE
The Cleansing and Clearing Out Process

"I am the true vine and
my father is the vinegrower.
He prunes away every
barren branch,
but the fruitful ones
he trims clean
to increase their yield."

(John 15:1-2)

23. TWO WAYS: CHOOSE ONE

THE classics in religious literature often present life as a choice between two roads, or two paths, or two ways.

As Psalm I puts it: you have the choice of being a tree planted near running water that gives its fruit in due season, whose leaves never fade or you can be like chaff, empty, a nothing, which the wind blows away.

Being rooted or being a drifter, something or nothing, full or empty? What will you be: A or B?

The Bible is filled with images that constantly stress two choices: wheat or chaff, wheat or weeds, good tree or bad tree, sheep or goat, narrow road or wide road, narrow gate or wide gate, good servant or bad servant, wise person or fool, building your house on rock or building your house on sand.

As Aldous Huxley put it, "The choice is always ours."

A priest I know used to love to give his "Apple Tree or Christmas Tree" sermon. He had read the image somewhere and turned it into a great sermon. The apple tree person is the type of person who gives blossoms in the spring, shade in the summer and apples in the fall. The Christmas tree person is the type of person who looks pretty, is decorated, and people put gifts at his or her feet. Then the priest would pause and add: "Of course you know that Christmas trees are either dead or artificial."

"The choice is always ours." Am I an apple tree person or a Christmas tree person?

We're back to the same idea presented earlier in this book: the image of the Golden Bridge. Which side of the Golden Bridge do I live on? "The choice is always ours."

The last two sections of this book will be divided according to those two choices. This section, Part Three, will zero in on the bad side of the bridge, the destructive side; Part Four will focus on the wheat side, the productive side.

"The choice is always ours."

It must be pointed out, however, that even though the focus of this section of the book will be on weeds that can be removed, we cannot rid ourselve of our past. We cannot deny reality. We've memorized it. If someone was abused as a child, he or she was abused as a child. If a spouse took off with a younger lover, he or she took off with a younger lover. If someone died, someone died. If someone hurt us, he or she hurt us.

Often we resist reality. We want to say, "It isn't so." Denial is one of the biggest road blocks on the way to the Golden Bridge. Denial is a paradox. We use it to deny the bad memory and in doing that we allow the bad memory to continue to hurt us more than it has to. The opposite of denial is acceptance. Acceptance brings the possibility of recovery. And recovery does not mean the erasure of the memory. It means learning to live with the past and not allowing it to paralyze our present and our future. A widow told me that she stopped going to a widows' group, because all they talked about was their dead husbands—some who had died 15 to 20 years earlier. She had done a lot of grieving, had great memories, and accepted the reality of her husband's death. Now she wanted to get on with life.

"The choice is always ours."

Where are you and where am I? Are you getting anything out

of this book so far? Am I challenging you enough? Writing this book has certainly challenged me. It has become more personal and autobiographical than expected. I didn't start page one with that in mind. How much have I revealed about myself? "The choice is always mine." Thanks for listening to me. Does anyone listen to you?

Listen to yourself. What's planted in the field of your life so far? Most of the things that happen to us, happen when we are half asleep. We sleepwalk till we are in our thirties. At least that's the time I woke up. That's the time so many of the people I have talked to woke up. We wake up as married with three kids and a job to do. We find ourselves saying to ourselves in the shower, "How did I ever get myself into this?" Then we begin saying, "Do I want all this? I took vows. I made promises. People are connected to me. I've made commitments. I've given my word to them. They have given their word to me. I am in a position of responsibility. My past means something. I can't deny it."

The first question that God asks in the Bible is, "Where are you?"

One of the best books that I ever read was *The Catholic Priest in the United States* (Psychological Investigations by Kennedy & Heckler). Back in April of 1967, the Catholic bishops of the United States voted to study the life and ministry of the American priests. Being a priest, it was an eye-opener for me. In its pages I saw myself. Most of us were immature and underdeveloped as persons. Many Catholic people would jest that you didn't need to do a study to find that out. But the study pointed out that we were more or less as mature or immature as the national average.

The kick was that it took a fall, a mistake, a dramatic experience, a great retreat, a tragedy, a death, or a rude awakening for someone who was an adolescent 35, 45, or 55 year old priest to move towards becoming someone whom God was calling to deeper faith, hope and charity. Upon waking, most were hit with the desire to catch up. There was a need to take "time out," to get updated emotionally, intellectually, and spiritually. The goal was to become a healthier and more alive person. The reality was that priests were ordinary people who were discovering the gift of choice and the need for affirmative action in their lives.

"Where are you?" How's your life? Are you still adolescent? Have you gone through any rude awakenings yet? Water that stands still, stagnates. Milk that remains in the refrigerator becomes sour. Bread that is not eaten becomes stale. Do you sense a power of choice in your life? Do you feel fully alive, giving all the love you can give, dying to make life better for the people you live with and work for? Do you agree with the poster slogan that says, "Not to decide is to decide?"

Life is choices:

> To decide or not to decide,
> To do or not to do,
> To sleep or not to sleep,
> "To be or not to be,"
> To listen or not to listen,
> To speak or not to speak,
> To grow up or to stay an adolescent,
> To marry or not to marry,
> To give up or to wake up and stick to
>   a marriage, a job, a family,
>   a vocation, and to work to
>   make it better,
> To love or not to love,
> To care or not to give a damn,
> To be honest or to B.S. my way through life,
> To bitch behind people's back, or to talk to
>   people whom I'm angry with,
> To give my word and keep it, or to break it
>   and not even think about the consequences,

To treat people as subjects or to use people as
  objects,
To be responsible or irresponsible,
To float or to know what port I'm headed for,
  using a compass, maps, a rudder and others,
To live life to the full or to die half-dead?

MANTRA: *"The choice is always ours."*

24. INTRODUCTION TO SIN

WHO introduced you to sin?

What was your first sin?

Are you dealing with any sins in your life right now?

Have you ever been tempted to break a trust or a secret or a vow, hesitated, then said to yourself, "The hell with the other person," and then told the secret, betrayed the trust, or broke the vow?

Looking at your life, have you ever overcome any sins? Was it a conscious battle or did the sinning in that particular way just end because of time or a change of circumstances? (For example, she moved away, or the cash box was moved to a new place?)

What is the worst sin?

How would you define sin?

What's the difference between temptations and sins?

Or are all these questions strange and foreign to you? Maybe you never talk or think about that three-letter word "sin" in the abstract? Or maybe you say things like the following when you're chatting at the bar or at a picnic with a beer in your hand: "I don't think there is any such thing as sin." "It all depends on how you look at things." "It's all relative." "Let your conscience be your guide." "What's wrong to one person is perfectly all right with another person."

Part Three of this book will challenge you to reflect and meditate upon the reality of sin, especially specific sins like: cruelty, greed, looking the other way, laziness, destroying other people's reputations, revenge, envy, sloth, lust, anger, pride, etc.

As stated several times already, we cannot undo our past. We cannot make what happened, not to have happened. "I am part of all that I have met." "We become what we eat." "We become what we read." "We become what we see." The choice is always ours to deny or accept our past. If we accept we are sinners, then we can use the energy we used for sin or for denial to nip and snip our weeds and not let them take over our garden.

Having said that, we can now point out that some weeds can be removed. If in the Parable of the Wheat and the Weeds, the enemy had planted the weeds in a field that wasn't being used, then they could be removed. Pulling them up would not have destroyed the wheat. So it all depends on how we are considering the mystery of sin. In Part Three of this book, I will be considering what is classically called, "The Purgative Way." It's the purging, the cleansing, the removal of the weeds, the illusions, the idols, the patterns, everything that is messing up individuals, their health, their relationships, and their environment.

Who introduced you to sin? Or haven't you realized its reality yet? Open your eyes and you'll see glimpses of hell. Open up the first three pages of the daily paper and you'll see pictures and stories of hell. Open your eyes and your ears and you'll see why Jesus the Rabbi came out of the carpenter shop.

God is against sin. God hates to see people hurting themselves or others. That's the way to see the reality of sin. But so many people deny hell and deny sin. We're lazy. We don't reflect. We don't think. In the meanwhile things go to hell.

The disciple of Jesus the Rabbi is called to think. We don't worry about sin till it hits home. We're like the people in the story of the Good Samaritan. We walk by sin. We deny it's there till it hits us. We begin to know there is such a thing as sin and evil when,

> —somebody steals our car battery,
> —breaks into our home,
> —we get fired because the new worker is younger, is in better shape than we are, and she opens the top two or three buttons of their blouse and catch the boss's eye,
> —our pastor takes off with the parish director of religious education and we know her husband and five

kids,
—a drunk driver smashes into our car,
—someone breaks into our car, steals our tape deck and unnecessarily wrecks the dashboard, pours beer on our front seat, and we discover all this as we get into our car leaving for an out of state wedding reception.

Sin is a cold three-letter word. It warms up when it hits home. It gets us hot and bothered when it's the reality of abused children, broken marriages because of infidelity, stolen wallets, ruined reputations, neglected parents, overeating, starving people, cold-silent-dead-marriages, and insensitive comments.

Who introduced you to sin? Have you ever been willing to take Jesus' invitation to go inside yourself and face your own sins?

When the rock throwers came to Jesus with the woman who was caught in the sin of adultery, Jesus wrote something in the sand. Then he said, "Let him without sin cast the first stone!"

Put down all those stones you throw at the reality of sin, your subtle way of avoiding looking at and accepting its reality in you. Sin exists. Sin is within. There are weeds in everyone's garden. And let's stop saying, "The weeds are always bigger in the other person's yard."

MANTRA: *"Let him (her) without sin cast the first stone!"*

25. CRUELTY: LOVE DAD

IT was her first weekend retreat. She sat there crying, trying to blurt out feelings of hurt that went back thirty-five to forty years.

Not happy with her efforts to tell what she was really feeling, she opened up her pocketbook and took out three pieces of paper: two poems and a "Dear Abby" letter from her local newspaper.

I began with the "Dear Abby" letter. I read it out loud to keep in touch with her sitting there in pain. An "Anonymous" wrote, "I am 30 years old, with two small children, and when I go home (I live in another town), I am treated like I am still 14 years old. My brothers and sisters (all older than me) and my parents, too, keep telling the same stories about how dumb, fat, sullen and miserable I was as a child. They all laugh like it was one big joke, and, Abby, those were the most painful years of my life. I am an adult now and want to put those painful memories behind me, but how can I when they keep repeating the same stories every year?"

Abby told Anonymous to see her brothers and sisters and parents individually and explain how she felt. If there was no change, then insist that you are not going to attend any more family get togethers.

I didn't know what to say, so I remained silent. "That's me," she said. "Everytime I visit my dad, I feel all kinds of anger and resentment swelling up inside me. And when I read that 'Dear Abby' letter, it all came back, especially the two poems I gave you." I looked at the poems. Both were short. She continued, "I was surprised at myself, remembering two poems from memory all the way back in my childhood. I jotted the poems down. Then I wondered if either my sister's or my autograph books could be found. That's where dad wrote the poems. I'm sure they are lost, because both my sister and I got married and we moved away. My sister saves everything, but I'd better not ask her. We never got along, anyhow."

She began to cry again. Then she added, "I guess the letter from

Dear Abby and the memory of those poems sums it all up. It's been a lifetime of anger against daddy dearest, always hearing his praises of her and his picking on me. She was always 'Daddy's Little Girl.' I was always, 'Go find your mother.' Or, 'Check with your grandfather.' And this garbage has been going on all my life. Just last week, I dropped in to see him with a gift for his birthday. As I handed him a card and a gift, he opened the card saying, 'Heard anything from your sister lately?' Then he tapped the birthday card, with his usual gesture of hoping money would fall out. He put the card down without even reading the note I put inside. Nor did he read the poem on the card. The flannel shirt I got him was looked at quickly, kept in its plastic, and then put down on the table. No word of thanks. Then he went back to watching his television program, leaving me standing there like a fool."

This time I deliberately stayed quiet.

"All this hit me last week, when I read that 'Dear Abby' letter," she continued. "My sister was always his favorite. Me, all my life, it's been second place. I guess that's why I've always struggled with this weight. My mom told me there was a time when I was thin. I got sick and the doctor told my mom to fatten me up. So all my life, it's been diets, jokes, exercise programs, poor self-image, and a whole tableful of 'feelings' that came with my overeating."

I looked down at the poems. "What about the poems? You said your dad wrote them?"

"Yes. I remember how I used to sneak up to my sister's autograph book. I would read over and over again the poem my daddy wrote to her and compare it with the one he had written to me."

The poem to her sister had four lines,

> You are daddy's little girl
>   right from the start,
> And there will never be another girl
>   to capture daddy's heart.
>   Love,
>   Daddy

After I read it out loud, she said, "See! It sums it all up. She was always his favorite and is till this day. Now, look at the poem he wrote to me." It was twice as long, but she said she had memorized it.

> Betty, Betty, you're no fool,
> whether you're in or out of school.
> But when it comes time for chow
> you eat and eat and never stop.
> You always clean the table top,
> so I hope you will stop it soon
> or else you'll puff up just like a balloon.
>   Love,
>   Daddy

We both sat there silently for what seemed ten minutes, not knowing what really happened and wondering what to say next.

Finally I said, "Could I write up what you just said? I'll change it around, so nobody will know who you are and where you live. Maybe your story will help someone else with the same problem."

She said, "Sure, but keep the poems as is."

MANTRA: *"God is our Father."*

26. "IT AIN'T FAIR!"

IT ain't fair: Haven't we said that inwardly many times? And haven't we also said it outwardly, when a big bump, or a big tragedy hits us?

Beneath the words is the basic assumption, "Life is supposed to be fair." Is it?

A few years ago, I attended a program called, EST. It was a two-weekend, three-other-evenings, 60-hours program, that tried to teach the 250 of us present, "What is, is." We would also learn, "What was, was; what isn't, isn't; and what wasn't, wasn't." They yelled that basic message that "what is, is," at us hundreds of different ways all through the program.

EST (which stands for either "It is" or Erhard Seminars Training) taught me the same basic message of the first step in AA: one has to accept reality. It taught me the first step of Buddhism: "Let go of desires." Don't we go through life wanting what isn't and denying what is? Don't we go through life wishing what happened not to have happened?

EST was considered rather controversial because of its confrontational tactics. They tried to get people to accept reality as it is. I found the program to be very helpful, especially when I heard person after person get up and tell us that they wished their parents hadn't abused them, or walked out on them as kids. I heard a lot of people sitting there stuck in their past. And after about 30 hours of that, I began to look at the person in my seat and to see how I was stuck in that same pattern.

Fortunately, I had great parents and a happy childhood. I grew up, the youngest of four, in a place very few people ever heard of: Brooklyn, N.Y. (I am still a Dodger fan. What happened, happened.) My problem wasn't in my childhood or my parents. It was in my inability at times to accept and allow other people to be who they are and the way they are. I had read somewhere, and even used it in sermons, a great quote, "The greatest sin is the inability to allow the other person their otherness."

Acceptance, allowing, admitting the reality of what is, is, and what was, was, takes time. It's a gift. Its opposite, wishing what isn't, numbs one to the present. It can also prevent one from forging a future that is different from one's past. We need to learn from the past, not get stuck in it, if it was a disaster area. Inability to accept the problems of the past is a set-up for the problem of resentment in the future.

Who said that life is supposed to work according to our script and scenario? Who said life is fair (and by fair we mean our idea of what is fair)? We are born where we are born, with the parents and family, or lack of family, that we are born into. We die, when we die, and where we die. We could try suicide to control our death, but even that doesn't always work.

Am I advocating a blind fatalism? No, I'm stressing a clear acceptance of the past and our present realities. The future is where we have the possibilities of new life. I'm advocating the wisdom of the serenity prayer: to accept the things we cannot change (our past), and to change the things we can change (some of our future). I'm advocating conversion and change where conversion and change are possible and called for.

On March 21st, my brother died of cancer. The medicine that he was taking to keep the swelling down in his brain was no longer working. Brain surgery was called for. I was trying to finish this book before he died. I didn't. That's reality. And compared to the reality of death, who cares? Dying at age 51 in our day and age is 25 years too soon. Plus we lost a wonderful person. He was a high extrovert, the life of the party type. He made a difference when he walked into a room. Some people come into your house like a fly and some people come in like a St. Bernard dog.

Was it fair that he died? Of course not. Should we compare his death to others? No. What we all have to do is to deal with his death and also what his life meant to each of us. His wife, Joanne, and their seven daughters have the biggest challenge. They and all of us knew and loved him, and also all of us who were known and loved by my brother, are moving into the future, grateful for having experienced someone who lived life to the full. Meanwhile, we deal with denial, hope, letting go, remembering, in the context of deep gratitude.

On a Thank You card sent to all who were with her and her seven daughters in his sickness and death, Joanne put my brother's picture, with these words underneath, "Thank you for knowing Pat..." Those who knew him, knew what we were feeling. Those who never knew my brother, missed out on a special person.

I had a long talk with him in February, a month before he died. We went for a car trip to Washington, D.C., to all our familiar spots. We got to know each other rather well as adults and could be very open. He knew he was dying. Before he even found out that he had cancer, he told me that he gave it a thought when he discovered he had a lump. During that car trip, he said things like:

—"Hey, this is happening to me. Cancer gives you a lot of time to think about life."

—"We all have to go sometime. This is my sometime, but not yet!"

—"You read in the paper about accidents and disasters and what people are going through. Now it's our turn."

—"I've had a great life. I'm glad I didn't wait till now to smell the roses. I've had it all."

—"I lucked out with Joanne. We've had a great marriage. And the seven girls are all grown up."

—"We've been here before with daddy dying of cancer and Michael dying (our nephew) of cancer at 15."

—"Obviously, I don't want to die. And I don't want pain. But what are you going to do?"

He was able to say things like that without going through EST. He experienced fear and he experienced faith. He was most grateful for the Catholic faith that our parents gave us—more by example, than by words. One of his main fears was being a burden on everyone who would have to care for him and the draining of energies that a long sickness might cause.

Being a realist, he watched himself getting worse, asking the doctors questions. He read all he could about melanoma. He began warning others about getting too much sun. Being a character, he used a magic marker to draw a diagram on his stomach, like a grid, to indicate where and when he would get his shots. His cancer doctor had never seen that one.

One of the choices that he consciously made was to try to help others deal with his dying. Over a year ago, he asked me, "You've dealt with this before as a priest, right?" Before I could reply, he answered his own question. (He always kidded about being the smarter brother.) "It seems to me, if I try to make it easier for others, it will be less pain for me." And that's what he did. People coming to see him during his many stays in the hospital over the past two years, would walk toward his room rather hesitantly. They would walk out cheered and laughing. He had the gift of needling people, even nurses and doctors who appeared with needles. One of the jokes to Joanne was the warning, "Wait till I become incontinent!" Sure, there was some denial in what he chose to do, but very little. He knew what was happening and he chose to think of others more than himself.

When he died, my brother's best friend, Marty, got a call from his son who was living in Israel for a year. David felt very lonely, because none of his friends knew "Uncle Pat." We had each other; he had no one around who knew the person he was crying for. And he told his dad that he was saying, "It ain't fair. It ain't fair," as he was crying. However, in the middle of the tears he started to laugh, because he remembered something my brother had done years earlier. My brother walked into the room, walked up to the television, and turned the channel to a ball game. He wanted to get the score. David, a little kid at the time, yelled out, "Hey, that ain't fair." And my brother, turned around and laughed at him saying, "Fair? Life ain't fair." And he went back to trying to get the score.

David never forgot that. Is life fair? Put down this book and think about that question. Is life fair? Have you had a fair deal? Should things be better for you? Should your parents, your teachers, your friends, have been better for you? What about sicknesses, car accidents, the tragedies in your life? Were they fair? What about the good news, the good things that have happened to you? Were they fair? Do you compare your life to others? If you do, why do you choose the people you choose for the comparisons? Ask others the question. It's a great discussion starter. And what about you? Have you treated others fairly?

People are not supposed to drive when they are drunk. Parents are supposed to take good care of their kids. Marriages are supposed to last. People who don't smoke should not get lung cancer. If I work hard, I should get this promotion. If we care for our kids, give them good example, go to church or the synagogue with them, then they should turn out right. Right?

When the car crashes, the marriage breaks, the star kid goes on drugs, the scoutmaster molests the kid, the dog gets run over by the drunk driver, we cry out, "It ain't fair."

Who said, "life is supposed to be fair?"

From EST I learned what is, is, and what isn't, isn't. From my brother I learned to live life to the full and help make one's death easier for those who love us. From the Buddha I learned that sorrow is part of everyone's life and one way to lessen it is to let up on trying to control life. From Jesus the Rabbi I learned that the cross is planted in the middle of our field. When we face sufferings and accept death, then Bad Fridays can become Good Fridays; Easter and Resurrection can be on the other side of the grave. From the Jesus of the Gospels I learned about a person who was scared, who cried, who wanted to run, but stayed after he prayed the great prayer of acceptance, "Father into your hands I place my life."

MANTRA PRAYER: *"Lord, help me to live to the full,*
but give me strength to accept life
when I have to run on empty."

27. REVENGE IS MINE

HOW do you get back at those who hurt you? How do you let those who treat you unfairly know they have treated you unfairly? How do you try to even the score? I try humor or silence, depending on the situation or the person. What's your strategy?

Take the writer, Nora Ephron. Supposedly, her book, *Heartburn,* is her way of getting back at her husband, who was allegedly having an affair while she was pregnant with their second child. At least that's the plot of the novel. Rachel Samstat, the heroine of the book, gets back at Mark by leaving him and Washington and heading for New York.

Did the book make Nora's husband, Carl Bernstein, cringe? How do you try to get back at those who hurt you?

Some people get hurt so badly that they hurt themselves even more in the process of trying to make those who hurt them feel guilty for hurting them. It feels kind of cold and cruel to say that, but I suspect that sometimes is the case. Are people who commit suicide trying to get back at those around them? What about the stories of adult children of alcoholic parents who become alcoholics themselves, or adults who abuse children, who themselves were abused?

We spend a lot of time, money and energy getting back at others. The strategies are many: wise cracks, breaking things, abuse, overeating, headaches, going public, being late, not showing up, etc.

The husband is out four nights a week, so his wife spends the weekend on a shopping spree. She feels that will teach him. That will even the score.

"An eye for an eye, a tooth for a tooth."

We play the role of "The Avenger" and "The Equalizer." We go through life always trying to keep the score even. "You can't let people step on you." We love Charles Bronson, Clint Eastwood or any actor who comes along to take their place in movies that show killers gunned down. "They had it coming to them."

"They had a 'Death Wish.' "

Jesus the Rabbi called for a stop to all the rock throwing. "You have heard the commandment, 'An eye for an eye, a tooth for a tooth.' But what I say to you is: offer no resistance to injury. When a person strikes you on the right cheek, turn and offer him the other. If anyone wants to go to law over your shirt, hand him your coat as well. Should anyone press you into service for one mile, go with him two miles. Give to the one who begs from you. Do not turn your back on the borrower" (Matthew 5:38-42).

People don't know or understand many of the messages Jesus gave, but they sure understand his teaching about turning the other cheek and they don't agree with it!

Rachel, in Nora Ephron's book, *Heartburn*, makes a great observation. Somehow it's nice to have bad people around—big sinners. It gets us off the hook. As she was leaving her husband, Rachel reflected "that it feels good, that there is something immensely pleasurable about moving from a complicated relationship which involves minor attrocities on both sides to a nice, neat, simple one where one person has done something so horrible and unforgivable that the other person is immediately absolved of all the low grade sins of sloth, envy, gluttony, avarice, and I forget the other three."

I hear her saying, "Let her without sin cast the first stone." And since we all sin, how can we cast stones. Yet we do. Read the book. It gives some good insights, using humor and pain, to show some of the things we do to each other.

If Jesus, the one without sin, didn't cast stones, how can we, the ones with sin, cast stones. That's what Jesus the Rabbi is trying to stop. Look at the Middle East, his own area. The principle that is running the power struggles is, "You bomb me and I'll bomb you. You escalate the terrorism and I'll escalate the retaliation."

Listen to what's going on. "The only thing that people understand is pain, muscle, power and the gun." "An eye for an eye and a tooth for a tooth.'' (Scripture experts tell us that this last principle was put in, because people were not retaliating equally. One person would be killed. The family or tribe that lost the son would wipe out a whole family to equalize the score.)

The cross is a gigantic red STOP sign. It's a gigantic billboard with the message, "Follow me and I'll teach you how to forgive." His message of forgiveness can be summed up in his words from the cross, "Father, forgive them for they do not know what they are doing."

The only revenge that works is forgiveness. The only revenge that stops revenge is forgiveness. We have to swallow our spit, instead of spitting back at our neighbor or our enemy who spits at us. That's the only way the cycle of hate, abuse, hurt, revenge, can stop. It's the way of the cross.

When will we ever learn that the person with revenge hurts himself as well as the person they try to hurt?

MANTRA: *Bear burdens, not grudges.*

28. IF-ING LIFE AWAY

IF you want to be a a Bible quoter, one of the easiest texts to remember is John 10:10. The numbers are easy to memorize: "10:10." I haven't seen it yet on a sign behind home plate at a baseball game or behind the goal posts at a football game for the television cameras to pick it up.

The text is a challenge and a promise. Jesus the Rabbi says, "I came that they might have life and have it to the full."

Look the text up. Actually, I'm only quoting the second part of John 10:10. The full text is worth looking at. "The thief comes only to steal and slaughter and destroy, I came that they might have life and have it to the full."

One way to steal, slaughter and destroy one's life is to "if" it away. In the last two meditations we have seen two other ways to destroy one's life: revenge and constantly thinking what's happened ain't fair.

Look at the quality of your life. Listen to what you're saying to yourself down there in your gut. Mark an X in the brackets before the following statements, if you have found yourself saying the statement on a regular basis:

1) [　] "If only I had waited, I would not have made such a stupid mistake."
2) [　] "If I had kept my mouth shut, I wouldn't be stuck here now."
3) [　] "If only I had stopped, when I knew I should have stopped, then this would never have happened."
4) [　] "If only I had listened, I would never have left school."
5) [　] "If only I had more money, everything would be all right."
6) [　] "If only I had more will power, I'd be able to overcome this problem."

108

7) [ ] "If I had more time, I'd exercise (read, do) more."
8) [ ] "If only I had a decent boss, this would be a decent job."
9) [ ] "If only I knew then, what I know now."
10) [ ] "If I hadn't taken that last drink, I would never have gotten drunk."
11) [ ] "If I knew these kids were going to turn out like this, I would never have had them."
12) [ ] "If only my parents hadn't done that to me as a kid, I wouldn't be the way I am now."
13) [ ] "If only God hadn't done this to me, I would not be in such a mess."
14) [ ] "If (s)he hadn't died, I'd be in much better shape than I am."
15) [ ] "If I had checked the mirror, I would have seen the damn car."
16) [ ] "If only I had studied more for the test, I would never have flunked (gotten a B, missed the promotion)."
17) [ ] "If only I started in time, I would have gotten here on time."
18) [ ] "If only the telephone hadn't rung (construction was going on, there was a traffic jam), we would have made it."
19) [ ] "If we hadn't moved so many times as kids, we'd be all right today."
20 [ ] "If only I hadn't marked X's in this book, because now somebody might see what I put down."

Doctor Smiley Blanton, writer and psychologist, after listening to people's problems for years (whether family, relationships, sexual, alcoholic, financial, etc.), began to hear two words underneath people's ways of describing their problems. "If only I hadn't gotten married..." "If only I had stopped..." "If only my kids..." If only we could hear how many times we use those two words, "if only." Next, to be positive, he also began to see that often the solution was to change those two words, "if only," to two other words: "next time."

Doctor Eric Berne, also a writer and a psychologist, said the same thing in almost the same words. He said that losers are always using two words: "if" and "maybe." Winners use three words, "Yes," "No" and "Wow."

Doctor W. Hugh Missildine, psychiatrist and author of *Your Inner Child of the Past* gives example after example in that book on how so many of us bring into our work, our relationships, our bed, childhood fears, loves, hates, losses, gains, neglects, achievements, attractions, complaints, punishments, rejections, guilts, feelings of worthlessness, overindulgences, being spoiled, etc. Our "inner child of the past" is often still feeling and suffering past things in the present moment, because something in the present moment triggers something from the past. We make decisions in the present moment, because of something from the past. Isn't that little two letter word "if," lurking in so many of our problems. Isn't "if," the heart of the matter?

Didn't Jesus come to invite us to leave home, to leave the past, to leave father and mother, to leave sin, to let go of hurts that still paralyze us, to stand up straight and walk, to put our hand to the plow and not keep on looking backwards.

Now all this is easy to say, but so hard to do. We're all sitting there with a lifetime of if's. I remember a mistake I made back in the 70's. I was facilitating a large assembly of religious. I booked the week-long program without realizing that I had also booked a retreat that weekend. That wasn't the mistake. The mistake was that I was scared to tell the organizer of the conference that I would have to leave early on Friday morning to get a plane home to start the retreat. He was quite unhappy when I asked if I could leave early. If only I had checked my schedule better. If only I had noticed the conflict earlier and told him. I can still feel my stupidity and my fears 15 years later. Reflecting on why I still lose energy over the experience, I realize that was the way I was as a child. When I got myself in a bind, I hesitated to tell my parents or teachers. If only I would learn. Lately I am learning how to say "Yes" and "No" and get away from the "if's" and the "maybe's." I went to that assembly 15 years ago, saying to myself, "Maybe it will end early and I'll be able to get to the airport in plenty of time." "If I play my cards right, I'll ask the organizer to telescope the final session and I'll be able to get home in time for the retreat." He said that I could leave early, but he let me know he was angry. Being a pleaser, I felt the tension, but also the pleaser's hope, "If only I could express my anger."

Jesus said that he came to give us life, and to give it to the full. If we go through life "if-ing," then we're throwing life down into the grave. Jesus said, "Say 'Yes' when you mean 'Yes' and 'No' when you mean 'No.' "

MANTRA: *"I came that you might have life and have it to the full."*

29. ENVY: EATING YOUR HEART OUT

CHRISTMAS DAY. How could anything go wrong? The whole family had box seats for the main event of the day. The two little boys, the star attractions, were driven in from New Jersey. They knelt down in adoration to the twenty presents before them. Each gift was clearly marked as to which present was for which boy. The signal was given and the grand opening began. The adults, modern Magi, smiled, cheered, rejoiced, felt great, especially at the moment their particular gift was being opened by one of the boys.

Christmas Day. How could anything go wrong? However, it happened. Just after the last present was opened, the fun ended. Each boy looked up and studied what his brother got. Scattered before them were a weird looking space man, a football helmet, a hockey jersey, a battery powered robot man with a laser gun and 16 other gifts. Without warning, each boy grabbed a toy that the other brother received. The wrestling match began with the basic cry, "It's mine!"

The adults were shocked and embarrassed. Like a little kid taking off his or her bathing suit at the beach, nobody was ready for what was happening. Neither boy hid his envy and his craving for more. Christmas Day or no Christmas Day, each fought to protect his artificial turf and if possible, to grab what he wanted from the other brother's turf.

Ladislav Mnacho said, "We're all really cavemen, squabbling over bigger or smaller chunks of meat."

Later on that same Christmas Day, an uncle, the silent one, was sitting in the corner. While the two were playing with their individual toys, he noticed that each brother kept glancing unhappily at his brother's toys. In fact, he thought neither seemed that happy with what they had received.

Those two boys are us. Obviously, we hide our selfishness and our unhappiness better than the little boys did. But don't we all fall into the trap at times, of not enjoying our piece of roast beef at a banquet, because the person across from us was delivered a better piece? Don't we envy the other person's yard and the upholstery in their new car?

This meditation is on the ugly sin of envy. However, it's very hard to separate envy from its brother, avarice (or greed). In an article in *Sign* magazine, Dorothy Sayers wrote, "If avarice is the sin of the haves against the have-nots, envy is the sin of the have-nots against the haves."

You have something that I don't have and it's eating my heart out. Envy deals with comparisons. Envy deals with not being satisfied with our own situation.

In the case of the two boys, the family saw their greed, their wanting more. But the uncle in the corner saw their envy, the unhappy spying and eying what the other brother had. That's envy.

Envy is a small person's sin. We become "the incredible shrinking woman" or man. And once more "if only's" arrive on the scene. "If only they would have given me that for a Christmas present. She always gets the best gifts." "If only I got a few breaks at work, I would have gotten the promotion instead of her." "If only I had the clothes, the figure, the looks, the schooling, the speaking ability, then...."

And so we sit there all alone, eating our heart out, instead of enjoying our roast beef.

And after eating our heart out, we become heartless. We begin trying to reduce those we envy down to our size. We become mean. Henry Fairlee, in his book on *The Seven Deadly Sins,* begins his essay on Envy with this point, "It has been said that Envy is the one deadly sin to which no one readily confesses. It seems to be the nastiest, the most grim, the meanest."

Do you accept that? Don't anger and lust and greed get better press coverage? But notice that he says that "no one readily confesses" it. Listen carefully to yourself and to those around you. You'll hear envy pop up from below our dark waters all the time. We make sudden shark attacks on others: smart remarks, snide shots, gossip, digs, etc. It's the sin of the cynic. It's the sin of the loser. It's the sin of the negative person. It's the sin of the comedian who uses her humor to put down the competition she fears.

Envy sells. We knew that sex did. But notice what the gossip magazines and papers do. They feature stories, whether true or false, of the stars in their weaker moments. Don't they work on our envy, telling us when the rich and the powerful mess up their lives? We pick up the gossip paper or magazine at the checkout counter at the supermarket to eat up stories that use in their headlines the magic words: "scandal," "affair," "secret revelation," "divorce," "drugs," "the daughter of," "the son of."

On the evening news we hear of a disaster in the Soviet Union—an earthquake—and sometimes a sneaky bubble of glee comes up from below our waters. The quarterback on the first place team gets injured...the perfect marriage in the parish breaks up...so and so's son gets picked up for having drugs. Sometimes one person's disaster is another person's joy.

Let's be honest. Don't we all subtly chip away or at least pick up a chip that has fallen from another person's statue, especially, when it's a statue that has fallen from a pedestal? The evil in us wants to reduce everyone to the lowest common denominator, because we feel smaller than the lowest common denominator. We figure we can stand taller on the ruins of those we toppled.

Envy is a stupid sin. We see it in the case of the two little boys, but don't see it in our own. Isn't that why Jesus the Rabbi kept throwing words into our pond, hoping that the ripples would eventually hit us, hoping they would sink into our depths.

Jesus told us that the man who had everything, who went to bed planning on building bigger and bigger barns, was going to die that night. He told us that the poor widow who put her two cents into the collection put in more than all the rest. They gave from their extra. She gave from what she shouldn't have given. He told us the story of the farmer who hired workers at various hours throughout the day. They were just standing around without any work. At the end of the day he gave everyone the same amount of pay. Those who began work first thing in the morning expected more, even though they had agreed to the regular daily wage. When they didn't get more, they complained. The farmer answered, "I do you no injustice. You agreed on the usual wage, did you not? Take your pay and go home. I intend to give this man who was hired last the same pay as you. I am free to do as I please with my money, am I not? Or are you envious because I am generous?" (Matthew 20:13-15).

The id, that word of Freud's, that describes the greedy and envious kid within us, is sometimes understandable in the little child. We're uncomfortable when little kids fight over Christmas presents, but we hope that corrections, discipline, hearing the word "no" will all help the kids to grow. We know the kid has to learn the reality principle, that we can't have it all, in spite of advertisements telling us that we can. Otherwise the child's ego will never develop properly. The kid will grow up, take on an adult body, but inside the id, the selfish kid will remain.

One of the nicest compliments that Marty, my brother's best friend, gave him was, "If you got a new car or a chance to go on a nice vacation, Pat would celebrate with you. And you knew when you walked out the door, he wouldn't say behind your back, 'What a showoff. Who does he think he is?'"

What about you? Do you rejoice when others rejoice? Are you happy when people get Christmas gifts that are different or "better" than yours? Or do you go through life as a small person, with a small mind and a small heart, never happy with your own gifts?

MANTRA: *Small minds live small lives.*

30. SLOTH: KICKING BUTT

SLOTH: even the word sounds like something is wrong with it. It's not a name manufacturers would give to a car, nor is it a nickname that any of us would like to be tagged with.

Sloth: a good word to describe laziness: but we don't use it too often, being too lazy to improve our vocabulary.

Sloth: laziness, poor service, sitting around and talking emptiness on endless coffee breaks, wasting time, keeping people waiting, not cleaning up after ourselves, not using our minds, vague spirituality, and a thousand and one other excuses for inertia. Such is sloth.

Sloth usually comes with "but's": "BUT I didn't know." "BUT I didn't realize you were waiting." "BUT I'm sorry." "BUT I didn't hear you say that." "BUT I didn't think anyone would notice." "BUT I didn't think they were killing the Jews." "BUT I never would have thought my kids would take drugs."

Excuses, excuses. We have to kick "but(t)": our own. That's the theme of this meditation. I hesitate to deal with sloth, because I know how often I put off till next week, what I know I won't do tomorrow.

BUT by writing about sloth, I hope I will give myself a good kick in the butt. I agreed to write this book a year ago, figuring I'd have plenty of time, BUT I found myself putting it off with excuse after excuse.

BUT deadlines make me finish things. BUT deadlines also kill me. I was this way all through school, and I still have not learned. BUT I get a lot done this way. BUT I deaden myself in the process—adding unnecessary stress on myself because of poor planning and lazy self-management. BUT I always did it this way.

So sloth kills. It's one of the seven deadly sins, along with anger, greed, gluttony, lust, envy and pride.

Turn off the television. Stop running. Step back and read a good novel like *Doctor Zhivago* by Boris Pasternak. It will make you think. He tells us, "We are born to live, not to prepare for life." Sloth tells us, "Buy the video movie of *Doctor Zhivago* instead. Omar Sharif is great. Julie Christie is beautiful. And start life tomorrow."

Jesus the Rabbi says, "Start life today." Jesus tells us that the meaning of life is to deal with today's worries and issues today. Feed the hungry and care for the poor, not out there, but here where you are.

Jesus urges us to be like The Good Samaritan. While walking down the road, he stopped to help the man who was robbed and left there half-dead. The two other persons who walked down the road before him were also half-dead. They didn't stop to help. "BUT I have to get home." "BUT I have to get to the temple to pray" (Luke 10:25-36).

Jesus urges us not to be like the Rich Man, Dives, who walked by the Poor Man, Lazarus, everyday, even though Lazarus was sitting at his doorstep (Luke 16:19-31).

BUT I don't know anybody who is poor and starving. BUT I could get mugged. BUT does it really help someone to give them handouts?

We're half-dead if we think that the Gospel is only talking about people in the Bowery, or starving in East Africa, or mugged in the streets. We're all smart enough to be lazy enough to avoid translating the Gospel for our own doorstep. Often the person who is hurting or hungry is next to us in bed or sitting next to us watching television. We use our brains to do crossword puzzles, but we don't use our brains to hear the words people around us are using to tell us about the crosses they are carrying. We're half-dead, half-blind, half-deaf. We don't hear the cries of the poor in our own family or next to us at work, those to whom it would mean an awful lot just to hear a two letter word beginning with "h" and ending with "i."

Sloth then is the label for the deadly sin that destroys life. And life is not an abstract word existing by itself out there. No, life is in us people, in trees, in plants, in animals. When we are lazy and irresponsible, we can destroy life. We can make a mess of nature and the environment. We abuse people, parks, public transportation, our air, etc. Sloth then brings hell to the here and now. Hell is the absence of life, the absence of care, the absence of concern for the physical, the mental and the spiritual.

The Physical

Let's start with the physical. Obviously, a person can be in great physical shape and still be quite lazy. Someone can jog two miles every morning and then come into work and do nothing. A person can be in top physical shape and be the laziest person in the class when it comes to thinking. A priest can run in the marathon and never pray, nor give us a spiritual thought from his depths. He could come home from his run and then serve us canned sermons.

Yet, taking a long walk, getting a good workout, doing aerobic exercises, should help clear the cobwebs out of our brain, uplift our spirit, as well as strengthen our body. To take a hike, go to the mountains, walk along the beach, walk around the block, is obviously a better use of time than a steady diet of junk food in front of a television watching soaps. Fresh air can give us a fresh outlook. How often do we sit around complaining to ourselves that nobody listens to us? The answer is simple: we have become dull and dumb. We're too lazy to stop and listen to ourselves and discover how boring we've become. How can we expect others to listen to us, if we don't even listen to ourselves. The first place to start then is to start with our bodies. We need to listen to our body screaming out, "Give me a break. Take me for a walk. Get me in shape. Stop filling me with all that junk." As they say in exercise classes, "Listen to your body."

The Mind

However, as indicated, sloth can also be of the mind, as well as of the body and the spirit, or in all three areas. In fact, we can keep running to avoid thinking or looking at our spiritual sides. We can also keep reading, to avoid thinking. As Seneca said back in the first century, "I think to myself how many exercise their bodies and how few their minds."

Look how many people think xeroxing an article is owning it. The machine has done all the work; we haven't done anything. I even cut newspaper articles up, so they can fit nice and neatly on an 8½ x 11 piece of paper, and then xerox them. Then I put it in my files, thinking that I've studied it. We go out and buy magic markers and different color pens to mark up our books. Wouldn't it be better to get out a blank piece of paper and jot down questions that come to mind from a book or an article, then discuss the questions, or rewrite what the author is saying in our own words? Wouldn't it be better to read one article five times, each time studying it, asking questions, wondering, than reading five articles once, without any thinking?

In the novel, *Doctor Zhivago,* Lara says something about Russia at the time of the Revolution that could be said of us here and now. "It was then that untruth came down on our land of Russia. The main misfortune, the root of all the evil to come, was the loss of confidence in the value of one's own opinion. People imagined that it was out of date to follow their own moral sense, that they must all sing in chorus, and live by other people's notions, notions that were being crammed down everybody's throat. And then there arose the power of the glittering phrase, first the Tsarist, then the revolutionary."

Isn't that us? We let the crowd, public opinion, ads, newspapers and magazines, do our thinking for us? Pollsters tell politicians what to say. We make jokes about it, but remain too lazy to think for ourselves. We become robots with buttons to be pushed. We join in criticisms about books, theologians, politicians, public figures, issues, without having read the book, met the person, or having studied the issue.

The Spiritual

And when it comes to the spiritual, we rattle off our prayers without thinking, watching our watches, wondering about yesterday or tomorrow. The priest in the front, the usher in the back, and the people in the middle, can all be present in body, but miles away from the church in spirit.

Too harsh? Too strong? Read this meditation five times and you be the judge. Or next Sunday, when you are in church, listen to the priest. Watch the people. See the kids standing in the back of church. What is your heart saying about the moment? Is it a moment of faith? Okay, we are not supposed to throw stones and we're not supposed to judge? Then be Jesus. Walk into church and sit down and see what he would see. Would he yell out, "My house is a house of prayer. You all seem to be a den of sleepers. Could you not stay awake with me for even an hour? I have come that you might have life and have it to the full."

Study the readings for the Sunday liturgy; what would you preach on? Take a good look at the parish bulletin; how would you put it together? Look at the local Catholic newspaper; have you ever studied it critically?

We go through life complaining that the other person is too lazy to take the garbage out. Take it out yourself: the garbage in your body, mind and spirit. BUT I didn't know it was my job?

MANTRA: *"Kick butt: take the garbage out."*

31. AVOID GREED IN ALL ITS FORMS

"AVOID greed in all its forms." That's one of the basic teachings of Jesus. It will be the mantra at the end of this meditation. Spend a week repeating that saying of Jesus the Rabbi to yourself: "Avoid greed in all its forms." "Avoid greed in all its forms." Reflect upon it. See how many different forms of greed you'll begin to notice.

Of course, start with yourself (another basic teaching of Jesus). Greed is a sneaky sin. If you don't watch it in yourself, it will get you while you're trying to collect "stuff"—while you are stuffing yourself with stuff. It's a slow, but deadly killer. Dorothy Sayers described it as "a narrow, creeping, pinched kind of sin."

She also described it as "an unromantic, unspectacular sin." She wrote that before modern theologians began talking about what is called "structural sin." And once you start looking at the structures of our world you can see spectacular examples of greed.

Take, for example, the horror of a large corporation and factory leaving a town. The owners blame the unions, saying that they were greedy. The workers accuse the owners of greed in moving the company, saying that they figured out that they would make more money by relocating with cheaper labor in another part of the country or the world. One structure then affects other structures, as in the domino theory, and soon local stores, restaurants, schools, churches, temples, clubs, etc., are all forced to make moves. Caution: human beings are present on the planet.

"No man is an island." We are all interconnected. No island is an island. It is interconnected with the rest of the area and the area is part of our world. Explode a nuclear bomb on one island in the Pacific and watch how it affects other islands. The United States annexed the Hawaiian Islands in the last century. Take a look at what has happened as a result. A nuclear accident on Three Mile Island affects all nuclear power plants throughout the United States, those in operation and those being built. A nuclear acci-

dent takes place at the Chernobyl power plant in Russia and the
story and the radiation cannot be contained. The countries of
Europe demand an accounting of what happened.

From where I am writing, I can look out my window and see
small hills and mountains on the other side of the Hudson River.
Here in Upstate New York we have green mountains all around
us. I've gone backpacking in Colorado, New Hampshire and Ver-
mont and I was amazed at all the beautiful trees we have. However,
it wasn't till last year that I discovered that we can destroy a lot
more than we already have. I went to a lecture at Bard College
given by Gary Snyder, the poet. He spoke about greed and how
we can save our environment. He spoke of a trip to Northern China.
The wood is gone. The houses are made of stone and brick. Around
the twelfth century, forests, with lots of oak trees, were cut down.
Erosion set in. Bare rock mountains appeared. Those forests are
lost from the planet for good. Today the people there thought that
the area was always that way. He also pointed out that the uplands
of Italy were once scenic forests of oak and pine. Around the second century A.D., there was a great need for lumber to build ships
for the navy. History repeats itself. We don't learn from our past.
Today we are still denuding mother earth. We are stripping and
raping hundreds of square miles of tropical forest in Brazil and
many other places on the planet. Because of greed, we are causing more and more deserts. Because of greed, more and more green
will be replaced by grey—grey bare rock—the color of the dead
moon.

Looking at structural sin then, prophets, preachers, poets, en-
vironmentalists are urging us to become more aware of what we
are doing. We not only need to look at trees and forests, but we
also need to look at business and the economy, the world bank
and the local bank, toxic waste and topsoil, water tables and the
oceans of the earth, nuclear arms and nuclear waste, acid and acid
rain, migrations and food supplies. Fewer and fewer prophets who
speak out on these and other issues are being considered ''kooks.''
The evening news and our newspapers are telling us about places

like Minamata in Japan, where mercury poisoning was dumped into their fishing waters. The result was not only damage to the fish, but damage to the nervous systems of the people who ate the fish. There are over 30,000 hazardous waste dumpsites in the United States. When toxic poisons seep into water supplies, when babies are born deformed, when enough people get cancer, then we have situations like "Love Canal" in Niagara Falls, New York. Two hundred families had to evacuate for good. When a "Love Canal" becomes a "Greed Canal," and we're living there, then we understand those who are screaming about our environment.

"Avoid greed in all its forms."

Don't we all love to play the game of "Monopoly," when we own Boardwalk and Park Place, have hotels on them, and also own half of the other good properties on the board? When we are in that position, we will even lend money to others, because that will keep them in the game. That will keep them moving around the board, increasing chances for them to land on our properties. We want to get richer and richer. We don't mind when it's our turn to toss the dice, because we have control of most of the money and most of the property. Those losing don't mind going to jail and losing three turns to throw the dice. It's no longer any fun for them. They want to give up. You just can't win when somebody else has a monopoly.

"Avoid greed in all its forms."

In *A Meditator's Diary,* Jane Hamilton-Merritt discovered in Thailand that it took an awful lot of meditating to experience why the Buddha said that greed and desire for money, titles, things, control, and power make us so unhappy. Isn't that the same message of Jesus? Greed is the cause of suffering. We have to learn to cut back, cut down, and cut out, not trees, but the accumulation of so many material things. E. F. Schumacher, famous for his message and his book, that *Small Is Beautiful* said, "While the materialist is mainly interested in goods, the Buddhist is mainly interested in liberation."

Advertisers counter with, "You can have it all." "Go for it!"

"You're on the way to the top." "Master the possibilities." Want people to know who you are? Use this credit card. Drive this kind of a car. Wear this label. Drink this wine or cooler or beer or scotch. Go to this restaurant. Use this perfume or cologne. Make this salary.

"Avoid greed in all its forms."

We want television sets with 200 channels, with a dish outside, so that we can impress our neighbors and get even more channels. We want a video recorder on top of a video recorder, so that we can record more and more video movies, etc., etc., etc.

Back in the last century Ralph Waldo Emerson warned us, "Things are in the saddle and ride mankind." Jesus said in the first century, "Do not store up for yourselves an earthly treasure. Moths and rust corrode; thieves break in and steal. Make it your practice instead to store up heavenly treasure, which neither moths nor rust corrode nor thieves break in and steal. Remember, where your treasure is, there your heart is also" (Matthew 6:19-21).

As someone said, "Too many necessities is the mother of tension." Will Durant adds, "We don't want a thing because we have found a reason for it; we found a reason for it because we want it."

Take the whole issue of having children. Obviously, people have children or don't have children for various reasons. Jesus comes along and says, "Avoid greed in all its forms." People want to abort that saying of Jesus when it hits home. People want to control Jesus on that saying. But like the trees being cut down in the past in China and Italy, like mercury and chemicals being dumped into the water, everyone had better ask what effect will our high incidence of birth control and abortions have down the line? The Catholic Church stresses that there is a problem with birth control, especially when greed is at the root of it.

Jesus said, "Let the children come to me." His disciples were trying to control them. Probably they had a long day and they wanted a break. They wanted peace and quiet and no kids around. In fact, they were trying to get rid of the kids. "Jesus called for the children, saying: 'Let the children come to me. Do not shut them off. The reign of God belongs to such as these. Trust me when I tell you that whoever does not accept the kingdom of God as a child will not enter into it'' (Luke 18:15-17).

We can learn more about life from raising children than from a new BMW or a new dog. We're dealing here with major value questions. We're dealing here with questions about the meaning and purpose of life. What's going to happen to the children of parents whose value system is stuff first, children second? A classmate of mine, a priest who works in the Dominican Republic, told me how much it hits him to see all the toys kids in the States get compared to kids in the Dominican Republic. "It's twenty dolls to one." Which kids are getting the best education—the best value system?

While sitting in the hospital room with my brother and his wife and their seven daughters, on two different occasions I heard couples say to my brother, and especially to my sister-in-law, "We thought you were crazy to have all these kids. Now we know how lucky you are." When my brother died, about 18 people were around his bed in the Washington Hospital Center, holding hands, and praying. Family and friends are certainly more important than things. Who is going to take care of the old people, when the old people didn't have young people, when they were young people?

I don't have any children. The old way of thinking was to say that someday I am going to have to appear before the judgment seat of God and make an accounting of the stewardship of my life. I am very aware that I have not brought children into the world. I know the command of Genesis, where God says, "Be fertile and multiply; fill the earth and subdue it" (Genesis 1:28). I have thought about all this. I miss not having children. The newer way of thinking is that judgment is now. I go before God in prayer now and give an accounting of my stewardship. A priest is called "Father"—and I hope that I have given to the people whose lives I have entered in the past 21 years, the love that I would have given to a wife and children. When I haven't, then I got too wrapped up in television and self-comfort, blocking new life (a form of birth control) or killing new life (a form of abortion) in both myself and others. And it has not been a one-way street. I certainly have experienced from the people I have met the love of wife, children, family and friends. Being human, I expect people to cry when they hear of my death. I expect people at my funeral.

What about you? Where are you on all this?

MANTRA: *"Avoid greed in all its forms."*

32. SHOULD I TELL HER?

ACT ONE
"In the Rectory"

SHE began with tears. "My daughter is for abortion. I have the feeling she's pregnant, but I was afraid to ask. Should I tell her?"

A bit confused I asked, "Tell her what?"

"Well, it's a long story. When we first got married I got pregnant and wanted to have an abortion and my husband said, 'No!' Wow, was I angry when he did that to me. I pulled out all the stops to make him feel guilty. For the first five months I was hell to live with. He wasn't pregnant. I had to give up my job and career. In fact, I had a better job than he did. But it was different then. The kids today have much more pressure than we did."

"Is this the daughter you're talking about?"

"Yes," she answered with a great smile. "It was the best move we ever made. She's a special kid. And now twenty-six years later, she tells me she's in favor of abortion."

It was one of those rare emotional moments I've run into as a priest—sometimes making my job fearful and at other times worthwhile.

She became quiet. She was biting her thumbnail. A few more tears came. Then she closed with a question, one really directed to herself, "Should I tell her what her father did for her?"

Then, as an afterthought, I said, "Did you talk to your husband?"

"Yes, I was thinking of that one. I don't know. It would kill both of them, I think. I need some time on that one."

ACT TWO
"Over the Phone"

"Hon, I talked to mom Sunday, but I couldn't tell her I was pregnant. And I couldn't tell her I wanted to abort. I just got nervous and said, 'I am in favor of abortion.' I think she knows."

"I didn't know you talked to her. Why didn't you tell me?"

"I know. But hon, this is all happening too fast for both of us. I just need some time to think."

She could hear his, "Phew" and then a long pause. Finally, "Well, you know how parents can't wait till they're grandparents. I just don't think they know how complicated life is today. Look, we got car payments, house payments, loan payments. And you're just beginning to find a niche in your company."

"I know, I know," she said, "but maybe this is what we're supposed to do."

"What? Okay, I know what you're saying, but I thought we agreed that we were going to wait a few more years till we started having kids."

"I know, I know, but what's more important? Work is work. Kids are kids. Damn it. A woman just can't win in this situation. Men have it so much easier."

"Honey, we just can't do this now. It's just not the right time."

Before she put the phone down, she said, "Let me talk to my dad. I could always talk to him. I'll ask him for advice."

ACT III
"Talking to Dad"

They hadn't gone for a good walk together in about three years. But here they were walking the circle that they used to take as kids on special occasions. He knew something was up when she called. His wife seemed worried when he mentioned her name last night.

With each step and each unfolding of her situation, he could hear himself saying, "Should I tell her? Should I tell her?"

"Look dad, I finally understand my job. College helped. But I needed these two years of experience to really get it down. If I quit now, I'll never have this opportunity again."

He was a good listener—but the question kept getting in the way, "Should I tell her? Should I tell her?"

"It's not that we don't want to have kids. But now is the worst time in the world. You understand. You and mom struggled all these years. And look how much it took out of you to get the four of us through college. I know, I know, I could have done more as the oldest to help. So we don't want to go through all that for us and our kids. We think it's better if we're more settled and when there is less pressure."

They were getting closer to the house. He said, "It's a beautiful day. Let's go around the circle again. There are a few things I want to talk about and there's something I never told you."

She got nervous at those last words—especially when she looked up and saw his eyes filled with tears.

MANTRA: *"How much more will your heavenly Father give good things to anyone who asks him!"* (Matthew 7:11)

33. GLUTTONY: GLUT, GUT

THIS meditation will be about gluttony—which means overdoing it with food and drink to such an extent that we do damage to ourselves.

My stress, however, will be on eating more than drinking. Thanks to Alcoholics Anonymous, other programs, and books, there are an abundance of good resources on alcoholism and drunkenness. By a narrow focus on food, I hope to be of better service to you, the reader, than if I wrote on a gluttony for alcohol, drugs and consumer goods, etc.

Recently, I found myself sitting next to an enormous person at table. The platters and bowls of food were passed around and he only half-filled his plate. As he began eating, he commented, "I don't eat that much." None of us had said anything before his comment; we certainly didn't after it. But did we say something with our eyes or other body language? Or did he expect a comment from a significant other from his past, standing over his shoulder (mom or dad)? I don't know. However, I found myself saying inwardly, "Fat people have to eat sometime."

I probably said that because of something that happened about a year ago. After lunch I went to our back storage room to see if I could find yesterday's paper. We also had cookies, pretzels and soda there. I walked across the carpeted floor and into the back room. Standing there was this big priest, putting two cookies in his mouth. Gesturing with a handful of cookies he said, "You caught me stuffing my face."

We walk into about 25 situations a day—$25 \times 365 = 9,125$. Most are forgotten by nightfall or by the end of the week. How come that one scene from years ago still stands out in my mind? I felt like I'd walked in on someone naked. Was he expecting me to throw stones? Does he go through life feeling guilty every time he eats snacks or "sneaks snacks"? Does he feel like a little kid caught with his hand in the cookie jar? What's his story?

The only thing I could say was, "Hi!"

As it settled in on me what had happened, I felt sorry for him. I am not the most sensitive person in the world when it comes to obesity. I hate to see people damaging their personal ecology and environment. However, I haven't walked in their shoes. I don't know their story. Were they rewarded with food as a kid? Did they get cookies to shut up? Did they get sweets and treats if they went to bed? Did they have fat parents? What's going on in their life?

What's going on in my life? What's going on in your life? Since this is a book on spirituality, it may be important to ask you to look at the place of food and drink in your life.

For clarity and order I'll divide the rest of this meditation into three parts:

1. What about Jesus and gluttony?
2. What about myself and gluttony?
3. What about growth in caring and sensitivity towards people who are dealing with gluttony?

1. *Jesus and Gluttony*

Jesus the Rabbi was accused of being Jesus the Glutton and Jesus the Drunkard. Yes, he ate and drank. Yes, he was concerned about food. He planned "get togethers" with food. He fed people who had come a long distance to hear him speak and were without food. He ate with friends, sinners, tax collectors and those outside the law (Matthew 11:19).

Jesus the Rabbi also fasted. He went into the desert for forty days. "During that time he ate nothing, and at the end of it he was hungry" (Luke 4:2). We don't know exactly what he looked like, what he weighed. Yet, I've never seen an image of him on the cross with a gut. His lifestyle, as outlined in the Gospels, suggests a man who was lean and trim. He was on the move, without house or home. Moreover, he warned, stop worrying, then, over questions like, "What are we to eat, or what are we to drink, or what are we to wear?" (Matthew 6:31).

Reading Jesus' comments about food, it seems that his stress was on what is called the "Middle Way" in Buddhism. "Virtue stands in the middle." However, the story of Buddha is different from that of Jesus. The popular tradition pictures the Buddha in his early life going from one extreme to the other: overindulgence to severe austerity. Not receiving peace and enlightenment in his ascetical period, he discovered the "Middle Way." He realized the need for obtaining strength from rice and other food. Thus the Buddha is often, but not always, pictured with a good belly. This is not to be taken as a movement back to overindulgence. His enlightenment was the "Middle Way." That is where we must grow in depth.

Jesus the Rabbi, without the "Buddha belly," also ate and drank. But he also told his disciples that there would be times of fasting. "The day will come, however, when the groom will be taken away from them; on that day they will fast" (Mark 2:20). In the meanwhile we should enjoy eating without being obsessive about it. And while we're eating, make sure we are aware of those who are without food. Invite them to eat with us. Feed the hungry (Luke 14:12; Matthew 25:35; Matthew 12:1-5; Matthew 8:14; Luke 7:36; Luke 19:5).

2. *Myself and Gluttony*

Find a quiet place where you can sit by yourself. Next, put a chair opposite you. Picture Jesus sitting there. Now, would he talk to you about your eating or drinking habits? Would he ask about your weight, shape, health? Or would he deal with other issues? There are no commandments like: "Thou shalt honor the thin and the slim," or "Thou shalt not have a large stomach before thee." But there are the commandments to love oneself and not kill oneself. We are created by God. We are God's temple. And

Paul came along and warned us not to make our belly our god (Philippians 3:19).

Here are some possible journal questions to get you thinking about gluttony in your life: How do you feel before you step on a scale? How do you feel about your eating patterns? What are your fears when you go for a good medical checkup? If your body could write you a letter, what would it say? Are you happy with the shape and health you're in for your age? Are you satisfied with your eating habits? Do you gulp down food or are you grateful for it, savoring and appreciating it? What are your drinking patterns? Alcohol? Coffee? Soda? Do you smoke? Write down the weight you think is healthy for someone with your frame. When it comes to talking and thinking about food, health and shape, are you balanced? Or are you obsessive, always talking inwardly or outwardly about inches to pinch, flab to fade, shape, exercise, food, diets, diets and more diets?

Many specialists on exercise tell us the practical advice, "Listen to your body." I would add, "Listen to your clothes." If you are overweight, lose ten pounds and notice not only your body, but also your clothes. If you don't exercise, why not? Have you given up on life? Are you killing yourself slowly? Move it.

3. *Others and Gluttony*

The third issue would be to look at one's attitude towards gluttony in others. The hope here would be a growth in understanding and sensitivity to others—and, if possible, to help where we can.

I remember attending a lecture on counseling. The speaker mentioned something that was so obvious that I obviously was missing it: "When someone comes in to see you with a problem, take a good look at their body. Start there. What kind of shape do they look like they're in? Ask them. Don't ignore the obvious. And if they are hoping to recover from some problem or tragedy, suggest starting with their body. Take walks. Get fresh air and exercise. Get a medical checkup. If they are out of shape, get them to tell you the best steps for improving their eating, sleeping, and exercise patterns.''

After that lecture, I began bringing into my retreat talks some comments about weight and overeating, taking care of one's health, while at the same time not being obsessive about diets, food, shape and exercise. It became obvious to me that the spiritual journey and the recovery journey should begin with the visible, the body, working on good eating habits, regular exercise, getting a good medical checkup—living a balanced life.

Well, I rarely receive feedback after talks, but after my comments about the body, eating, diets, being overweight, etc., people came up to me and said, ''Cut it out. You're off on fat people.'' Being six feet tall and weighing about 170 since 1960, I suppose it was easier for me to make comments about weight.

Those comments made me think. I don't like anyone to grab my ''love handles'' or ''pinch my inches.'' In fact, when I see friends coming, I pull in my gut before they can poke or grab me. I'm beginning to see I was insensitive. And maybe that's where we all should begin: to become more sensitive to overweight people.

And to become more sensitive, picture fat kids as they have to face the arrival of the yellow school bus, Monday through Friday. Feel the daily hurt from the ''fun'' remarks that they hear as the bus pulls up to their stop. Then there is the inside of the bus, the going down the aisle. And that's just going to school. What about all day in school and then going home on the bus? Remarks, jabs, jokes, grabbing, pinching, have got to make it a long day for fat people—adding more than enough stress to their lives. Life is a stress test. Why add to it? Did the priest with the cookies in the back room have to take a yellow bus to school when he was a kid?

Our society puts too much pressure on all of us to be in shape, to be slim and trim. The movies, television, magazines, present models who are in "perfect shape." No wonder we have young women with anorexia and people addicted to amphetamines which they took to lose or control weight. People with weak egos, a poor self-image, and fifty pounds too much, aren't helped by all this stress to jog, lift weights, join an aerobics class, drink light beer, eat yogurt, so as to be in perfect shape.

The pressure doesn't stop there. Fat people not only hear remarks from people on yellow buses and on television. They also hear them from their greatest critics: themselves. You hear them sniping away at themselves all the time. That's outwardly. Imagine what's going on inside: swallowing garbage from themselves for failed resolutions. Eating because things are eating them up. Imagine how they become gluttons for punishment.

An article back in 1979 in *The New York Times* opened my eyes to another factor about overweight people that should get them off the hook from smart remarks—but not the need to take care of the problem of being overweight. Jane E. Brody said: "While obesity afflicts only 7 percent of the children of parents who themselves are normal in weight, the research shows that 40 percent of the children with one fat parent and 80 percent of those with two parents also become fat. But this can result from an environment that fosters overeating as well as from inherited tendencies. Studies of adopted children and identical twins reared together and apart have shown somewhat conflicting results, but the preponderance of evidence indicates that environment plays a stronger role than heredity. A genetic predisposition to be fat will be expressed only if the environment in which the person is raised permits it. A study in England disclosed that the pets of fat people are twice as likely to be fat as the pets of thin people."

Hopefully, all these comments will make all of us more sensitive to the issue of gluttony in a world where there is enough food, but a critical problem in getting it distributed to everyone. Hopefully, we will be more sensitive and less critical of overweight people. When possible, maybe we can help people to see a good doctor, join Weight Watchers or Overeaters Anonymous or some other group. Friendships and caring call for such support. Henry Fairlie said, "Gluttony makes us solitary." People go to the back room to eat. Maybe that's where we have to meet them and say more than "Hi!"

MANTRA: *"Life is more important than food." (Luke 12:23).*

34. LOST IN LUST

WERE you ever "in lust" and you thought you were "in love"? This meditation will attempt to portray both attitudes and obviously stress love instead of lust.

The contrast between these two is brought out in a good example by Alphonsus Jansen in his book, *The Meaning of Love and Marriage*. This book, put out in paperback in 1966 by Divine Word Publications, may be difficult to find today. But, if you get your hands on one, you'll have one of the better books on the subject of love and marriage.

The example is this: picture a girl at a swimming pool. A boy sees her, likes her looks, and swims around her a few times. Then he starts talking to her. He finds out that her name is Ann, that she works in a hatshop, that her mom is a widow, that she has two brothers, and that she loves the movies. Seeing her the following week, he says to a friend, "Hey, there's Ann!" Another boy also sees her at the swimming pool. He makes no attempt to know her. Instead, he makes comments about her body, probably viewing her through sunglasses. Suddenly, he has sexual temptations. He fights them, suppresses his feelings, and then changes his thoughts to something else.

In a similar situation, how would you react? We do have a choice. Were you ever "in lust" and you thought you were "in love"?

Before answering, pause and think more about the question. Look back on the story of your life. Maybe do some journal work on it. Then ask yourself this: "Do I see people as subjects or objects?" To see people as subjects means to know their name, to listen to their story, to find out about their feelings, thoughts, dreams, hopes, hurts, and fears. To see people as objects means to view them as problems, temptations, cases. It means looking at sex as plumbing and parts, as something to use, abuse, or avoid.

Perhaps we do not reflect very often on what we are seeing, saying, or doing. "Father, forgive us for we know not what we

137

are doing.'' Who of us could stand up in public and tell our sexual standards? Without blushing, that is.

Looking back, I must admit that very often I have kept my mouth shut when it came to teaching or preaching on sexual morality. I have had to do a lot of thinking, praying, growing, talking, reading—or, in other words, a lot of homework—about all this. I've found out that a lot of other people, priests included, have been like me: standing back, making mistakes, avoiding the questions, and smiling so as not to offend others. We didn't want to appear old fashioned, out-of-touch, or out-of-date.

And as we kept quiet, a lot of wrong things were happening. Over 20,000,000 babies have been aborted in the United States since abortion was legalized in 1973. We hear people scream about preserving endangered species of whales and seals, but what about the tiny embyro? Make an embyro an ''it'' and you can ignore ''it.'' The research and statistics on the sexual abuse of children is just beginning to become known. But perhaps the full extent will never be known because of the terror such children feel toward the bigger people who abuse them. Still, some numbers are emerging. For example, at a talk given by a specialist who works with abused children, I heard that perhaps one out of every five girls and one out of every five to ten boys were abused sexually. And who are the abusers? We tend to make ''them'' the pervert who stands by a school-yard fence. But abuse by strangers accounts for only eight to ten percent of the cases. The other cases? Forty-six percent of the time, the abuser is a member of the family: a father, mother, grandfather, uncle, or brother. Forty percent of the time, the abuser is someone well known to the child: a friend of the family, teacher, clergyman, doctor, coach. The specialist I mentioned said that the stories of these children are horrendous. They are some of the best kept worst secrets in the world. And yet, when the child breaks the ''secret'' all too often there is still denial and a refusal to listen. Treat a person as an ''it'' and you can abuse ''it'' physically, sexually, verbally.

While we kept quiet, other wrong things have been happening

as well. Consider what happens when there is divorce in a family. The two who had become "one flesh" are torn apart. And often the flesh of their flesh, their children, are also ripped apart. And what about couples who try to force fit each other and their families into their work and social schedules, as if persons were "things" who could be wedged into a time-slot? What about the untold horror stories that happen in some homosexual situations—or with runaways or child prostitutes? Treat people as "its" and you can ignore a lot.

Does any of this jar you? If it does, that's a good sign. People who are "subjects" are moved by what they are subjected to, and what they subject others to as well. We need to be moved by all these matters; we need to think about these questions. We need clear, healthy thinking about our sexual morality.

But where do we start? It seems the majority of people are not listening to the Church, so whom should they listen to? For Christians, the obvious place is to return to Jesus the Rabbi. Listen to what he has to say. Jesus teaches a morality that is quite strict. For him, people are treated as persons. With him, we are allowed to make mistakes. Rocks are not to be thrown. Yet, we are also told not to sin again. And if we hurt ourselves once more? Then we can also be forgiven once more, and once more again, and seventy times seven times.

I could end here. But, since this is an important topic, I would like to make a suggestion that has been very helpful to me. It's this: go to the local bookstore and buy a copy of C. S. Lewis' *Mere Christianity*. It came out during the Second World War, and is now a classic. Macmillan put it out in a paperback edition in 1960 and keeps printing it.

In that book you will find a remarkable, clear and precise presentation of the teachings of Jesus Christ. Regarding chastity as opposed to lust, the teaching is rather exact. Lewis presents the old Christian rule: "Either marriage, with complete faithfulness to your partner, or else total abstinence" (p. 89). He advises not to build a marriage on feelings alone, as in the feeling of "being in love," because feelings don't last. If you want marriage and love to last, then build it on justice, a good match, family, true love, duty, etc. He writes, "If people do not believe in permanent marriage, it is perhaps better that they should live together unmarried than that they should make vows that they do not intend to keep." For Lewis, sexual intercourse is a very serious experience, having transcendental repercussions whether one accepts them or not. Whether a person is with a spouse or a prostitute, both are affected eternally. "The monstrosity of sexual intercourse outside of marriage is that those who indulge in it are trying to isolate one kind of union (the sexual) from all the other kinds of union which were intended to go along with it and make the total union." He spells this thought out more powerfully in his book, *The Four Loves,* in which he describes a lustful man prowling the streets in search of a woman. "Strictly speaking, a woman is just what he does not want. He wants a pleasure for which a woman happens to be the necessary piece of apparatus. How much he cares about the woman as such may be gauged by his attitude to her five minutes after fruition (one does not keep the carton after one has smoked the cigarettes)."

You can prowl too, if you think of people as "its." Were you ever "in lust," and thought it was love? Or were you ever "in love with love" and thought of the other as simply the means? Or have you ever experienced an other as a person? Now, that is where real love can begin.

As mentioned, C. S. Lewis is quite serious about sexual morality and Christian marriage. He once said that if you don't agree with the Jewish-Christian tradition on these subjects, then don't blame the synagogue or Church, fight with their founders.

One of Lewis' classic examples concerning his attitudes about sexuality is found in *Mere Christianity.* It's about a "strip-tease" show for food: "You get a large audience together for a strip-tease act—that is, to watch a girl undress on the stage. Now suppose you came to a country where you could fill a theatre by simply bringing a covered plate on to the stage and then slowly lifting the cover so as to let everyone see, just before the lights went out, that it contained a mutton chop or a bit of bacon, would you not think that in that country something had gone wrong with the appetite for food?''

Before ending the chapter on ''Christian Marriage'' in *Mere Christianity,* Lewis writes: ''If you disagree with me, of course, you will say, 'He knows nothing about it, he is not married.' You may quite possibly be right. But before you say that, make quite sure that you are judging me by what you really know from your experience and from watching the lives of your friends, and not by ideas you have derived from novels and films. This is not so easy to do as people think. Our experience is coloured through and through by books and plays and the cinema, and it takes patience and skill to disentangle the things we have really learned from life for ourselves.''

Later in life, Lewis was to marry an American woman, Joy Davidman. At first, they were good friends. When Joy and her sons were asked to leave England, perhaps because she had flirted with Communism in the 1930's, Lewis married her so that they would have British citizenship. In his words, the reason for the marriage was ''a pure matter of friendship and expediency.''

The friendship and expediency turned to deeper and deeper love. In Walter Hooper's book, *Through Joy and Beyond,* Lewis is quoted as saying, ''I never expected to have in my sixties the happiness that passed me by in my twenties.''

Unfortunately, their marriage lasted only four years. Joy had her ups and downs with cancer and sickness and in caring for her, Lewis discovered the heart of love—serving another. We already know what C. S. Lewis thought the Christian teaching on marriage was. In his powerful book, *A Grief Observed,* we can find out what he felt about the experience of being married. The book is a collection of his feelings in his missing of his Joy. Listen to these powerful love words,

   ''One thing, however, marriage has done for me. I can never again believe that religion is manufactured out of our unconscious, starved desires and is a substitute for sex. For those few years H. (Joy) and I feasted on love; every mode of it—solemn and merry, romantic and realistic, sometimes as dramatic as a thunderstorm, sometimes as comfortable and unemphatic as putting on your soft slippers. No cranny of heart or body remained unsatisfied. If God were a substitute for love we ought to have lost all interest in Him. Who'd bother about substitutes when he has the thing itself? But that isn't what happens. We both knew we wanted something besides one another—quite a different kind of something, a quite different kind of want. You might as well say that when lovers have one another they will never want to read, or eat—or breathe.''

MANTRA: *"Love one another as I have loved you."*

35. YOU GET ANGRY, DON'T YOU?

DOES everyone get angry? Does everyone get angry equally in equal situations? What are the best ways of dealing with anger?

Recently, I drove down to Maryland to see how my sister-in-law was doing after my brother's death. While she and my nieces were at work, I began writing this meditation. I wanted to cover the seven deadly sins as some of the weeds that grow in our field. I only have anger and pride to go. I asked my niece, Margie, and later my niece, Jeannie, about anger and how they saw themselves and others dealing with it.

Margie gave me the three questions that I began this meditation with. Jeannie pointed out that I was the type that never gets angry. "Last night," she said, "you came up to go to sleep and I was working on the computer in the room where you were to sleep. You said, 'Relax!' and told me to tell you when I was finished and that you would be downstairs watching television. Some people would get mad and frustrated because it was after midnight and they wanted to get to sleep."

She had pinpointed me well. In self-awareness tests I always came out as "The Pleaser" or "The Teddy-Bear" or "The Stuffer" or "The Martyr Who Suffers in Silence."

How about you? When things go wrong, when your expectations are not met, when your values or your feelings are trampled on, how do you react? For example, you're looking for a parking spot at the shopping center at the hospital. A car is about to pull out. You're there first, so you signal to the driver that you'll pull ahead to let them out. You pull up. They pull out. Another car arrives and shoots into the spot. How do you react? The couple next door have a daughter with a loud stereo. How do you react at one a.m., when you can't sleep because of the loud noise from next door?

Repress or express? What's your style? Some people anger in and some people anger out. When your "wrong button" is pushed, are you like a scratched match, or do you silently and slowly release acid into your gut? Are you assertive or non-assertive?

After a few discussions with my nieces, Margie and Jeannie, having read several books and articles on anger, I came up with lots of suggestions on how to deal with one's own anger and how to deal with other people when they are angry.

When You're Angry

1. Realize it's absolutely normal and healthy to feel anger. When you feel angry, at least begin by admitting it to yourself. As they say about sexual feelings, "When you're hot, you're hot; when you're not, you're not."

2. If possible, take a spot check to see if you can figure out what caused it. You might feel anger toward someone who is watching a movie on TV when you wanted to watch a football game. On reflection, it could be the remark they made about you at supper three hours or three years earlier that's the real cause of your anger.

3. If it's a person that you're angry with, would you get angry at every person who did this to you, or just this person?

4. Is the situation you're angry with something you should get angry at? Is someone being hurt? Is there an injustice?

5. The key issue is not losing your head or your freedom. Obviously, this is the heart of the matter when it comes to anger. If you can, ask yourself whether you want to say something or not? Why live life by reacting to it and letting other people control you? Why not try to act after a free choice. To express or not to express your anger in this situation: that is the question.

6. If you choose to express your anger by saying something to another, try to be constructive, not destructive. Don't attack. Assert. Admit your feelings of anger about what seems to have happened. For example, you got a speeding ticket and you told one person about it and then they bring it up at the din-

ner table. Later that night, when you're alone with that person, you say "I'm not sure what's going on, but I think it fair to let you know I've been feeling angry all evening. The comment at supper about my speeding ticket ticked me off. I'm very sensitive about things like that." Hopefully, words like that start communication. Why arrive at the scene of the discussion with aircraft carriers and destroyers?

7. If you choose to remain quiet, then don't express your anger with a silent cold shoulder, sleeping in another bed for a week, banging doors, lateness, or other forms of passive aggression.

8. If you choose to remain silent, make sure you don't do damage to yourself with higher blood pressure, colitis, skin problems, depression, sickness. These too can be unconscious passive aggressions against another or yourself. A while back the literature on anger was all for expression. Then researchers and observers found out that venting your anger can make it worse at times. Sometimes, those who blurt things out without thinking, burst out with more anger than they knew they had or wanted to express.

But those who hold it in can keep on getting angrier if they keep on talking and repeating to themselves what is bugging them. Everyone needs to learn what works best for them in conflict situations. If they can calmly talk to those they are angry with, great. If they can't, perhaps the best solution would be talking to a friend or an objective third party, not to ruin the reputation of the one you're angry with, but to ventilate or to clarify your feelings about what you think happened.

9. Make sure you are living a balanced life—enough sleep, recreation, work, prayer, walking, exercise, etc. Walk before you talk.

10. And that leads to one of the oldest suggestions about anger. It's the one we all know. Count to ten. Thomas Jefferson said, "When angry, count to ten before you speak; if very angry, a hundred." Mark Twain said, "When angry, count four; when very angry, swear." Athenodorus Ananites, who died

around the year eight A.D. said, "When you're angry, say nothing and do nothing until you have recited the alphabet."

When the Other is Angry

1. Once more, get in touch with your own feelings when you're with someone who seems angry. If you're nervous or uneasy, begin by telling yourself what you're feeling and thinking.
2. If you are a "Teddy Bear" or "A-Peacemaker-at-All-Cost," don't try to water down the other's feelings. Shut up. Let them speak their piece or peace. Don't try to say things like, "You're really not that angry, are you?"
3. At an appropriate time and in an appropriate way, if feasible, let the other person know you know they are angry.
4. If you're at fault, and if possible, admit it. However don't admit it to shut the other up or to make them feel guilty for getting angry. Do it to try to right the situation, if that's what is called for.
5. If the scene and the time are bad, see if you can set up a better place and time. For example, kids could be present, and they might not be ready for what's being said. Don't do this to manipulate the other, but to communicate better.
6. Don't deny you have feelings and a brain. If the other person's reaction doesn't seem to "fit the crime," ask yourself or the other, "Are you saying what you're saying or are you saying something else?"

Styles

In talking with Margie and Jeannie and also in reading the literature on anger, I realized that everyone does not get angry at the same thing in the same way. A group of people are at a restaurant. The food is slow in coming. Finally, the waitress arrives with the main course. "Boom!" She drops the whole tray of food and the result is a mess and at least fifteen more minutes of waiting. One person angrily yells for the manager. Another jumps up to help the "poor" waitress!

My nieces told me of a married couple that they know. He comes from a family where anger was freely expressed. She comes from a family where anger was never expressed. When they had their first fight, she thought her marriage was finished. In talking about it afterwards, the couple began to laugh. In fact, it became part of their repertoire of stories about themselves, their marriage and their families.

What about your background? Did your parents argue and disagree in front of you? If they did, was it communication or castigation? Was their constant yelling a long period of arctic silence? Were there good powwows when trouble or misunderstandings arose? A father might yell at the first kid he sees in the morning when he discovers that the milk was left out all night. He might be too busy or too lazy to ask questions. A teacher might pick a fight the first day of class to establish her or his authority. A husband might not say a word for three weeks to get back at a wife who has decided to attend a series of evening talks at a local college. I know someone who always—ALWAYS—sends her food back angrily to the kitchen whenever she goes to a restaurant. Us "Teddy Bears" sit there with trembling tummies every time.

What's your style? If someone video taped you for a month, what would the reviews say about you? "Teddy Bear" or "Shark?" "Lion" or "Lamb"?

Sinful?

By now it should be obvious that it's normal to feel anger. In fact, we ought to get angry at injustice and evil. We ought to become indignant when people damage people or our environment. When people are used or abused, we should not only feel anger, but the anger should move us to action.

We have all heard sermons about just anger. We have heard how Jesus got angry when he walked into the temple in Jerusalem and saw what had been a house of prayer changed into "a den of thieves." He got angry at the Pharisees when they got angry with him for curing someone on the Sabbath (John 7:23; Mark 3:5; Luke 19:45-46).

But Jesus the Rabbi also warned us about the kind of anger that destroys people, places and things. Anger can destroy family and friends. He warned us about anger whose roots are envy, greed, jealousy and the other deadly sins.

Anger is sinful when pharisaism, bigotry and prejudice appears, when we refuse to face our sins and shadows and project them onto individuals and groups.

Anger is sinful when we have become, "The Angry Young Man or Woman" or "The Bitter Old Man or Woman," who uses anger to scare, bully or manipulate people. We have all met people who always seem to be angry at anything and everything. They are the desk bangers, the horn beepers, the finger givers, the party poopers, the meeting ruiners and the hope destroyers.

Anger is sinful when we take out our anger and frustrations on children, the helpless, our own bodies, dogs, cats, furniture, doors, etc. We overdrink or overeat because we're in conflict with someone we are scared to talk to. The boss yells at us so we yell at our kid who is having a catch on our front lawn as we arrive home. "Why are you so damn lazy! I told you to cut the grass five times in the last four days. Put away the football and get out the lawnmower!"

Anger is dangerous on the highway. Temper tantrums can cause serious accidents when we're furious for people driving too slow, or staying too long in the passing lane, or refusing to lower their high beams.

Anger is wrong when we let ordinary mistakes by others trigger extraordinary outbursts from us. For example, we stayed up too late the night before watching television. The next morning we go to work tired and on edge. We're miserable the whole day.

Our eyes become magnifying glasses. Little bumps become major accidents. For example, we get ourselves into money troubles because of trying to live beyond our means or we gamble or go out too often to expensive restaurants, and the pressure gets to us. For example, college kids get angry at teachers for giving them poor grades. The truth might be that the kid didn't study, spending a whole semester majoring in partying.

Anger becomes even more deadly when it moves into our minds and we start planning revenge, when we become so obsessive with getting even with another that we lose control of our life.

And anger is wrong when we refuse to forgive. Read "The Story of the Prodigal Son." The father forgives his son for making a mess of his life, wasting money, perhaps ruining the family name, and causing him anxiety, not knowing where he was and what he was doing. The older brother refuses to come into the house to welcome his lost brother. Jesus the Rabbi describes the older brother as "angry" (read Luke 15:11-31). To this day we don't know if he ever calmed down and welcomed his brother home.

The New Testament also has several stories where people grew angry at Jesus because he was good. Haven't we all experienced anger coupled to jealousy and greed: when somebody we know wins something or does something great. We express our anger by starting nasty rumors, or sneaky innuendos. "It was fixed!" "She's just showing off."

The New Law that Jesus preached is the call to start with ourselves, to clean the inside of the cup, to pull the weeds out of our field. The call is to deal with anger through love. To turn the other cheek and to walk the extra mile. Our patience and calmness is the only way to stop the vicious cycle. Fighting begets fighting. Raise your voice and listen to how the other person's voice is raised. Get back at someone and expect retaliation in some form any day now. Red is the color of anger. It's also the color of the STOP sign. The cross is the red STOP sign where Jesus tried to *stop* anger and hatred by love and forgiveness. His hope was that we would see how anger and hatred destroy people—those who spit and curse and those who are hurt. His hope was that by spending some time under the cross we too would look at our own anger, hatred and resentments and say, "It is finished."

MANTRA TEXT: *"If you are angry, let it be without sin" (Ephesians 4:20).*

36. PRIDE: THE SNEAKY SIN

True or False Test

Here are five questions about the sin of pride. Write the word "true" or "false" in the blank space before the statement, based on whether you agree or disagree with it.

1) _____ "The worst of all sins is pride."
2) _____ "Pride is growing in everyone's field."
3) _____ "Pride is so bad that people don't notice it is in the center of both their hearts and everyday lives."
4) _____ "Pride is the sneakiest of all sins."
5) _____ "Pride is the hardest sin to admit."

True Answers

Being a sneak, I'm sure you noticed that the five statements given above were worded in a way to try to get you to answer "true" to every one of them. People taking tests want to get all the answers right. We hate to be wrong. And in that human dynamic of wanting to be right, we can see the very roots of pride. And what's worse, there is an evil quirk in us that makes us love it when we're right and the other person is wrong. That's full grown pride. (Agree or disagree? True or false?)

Pride is the worst of all the sins as well as the sneakiest. In C. S. Lewis' book, *Mere Christianity,* the chapter on "pride" is entitled: "The Great Sin." "According to Christian teachers," he writes, "the essential vice, the utmost evil, is Pride. Unchastity, anger, greed, drunkenness, and all that, are mere fleabites in comparison: it was through Pride that the devil became the devil: Pride leads to every other vice: it is the complete anti-God state of mind."

Pride: Above All, Me

The Bible starts off with God creating all, "and all is good."
The Bible starts off with God creating Man and Woman, "and
all is good." The Bible starts off with Man and Woman trying
to be equal with God, "and all is not so good."
Pride then is the first sin. It's the first sin of the devil. It's the
first sin of humans. And the babies of the world start off by screaming, "Me! Me! What about me?"
The first commandment has to be the one they came up with:
"I, the Lord, am your God, who brought you out of the land of
Egypt, that place of slavery. You shall not have other gods besides
me" (Exodus 20:1-3).
We break that commandment every day. We make ourselves
or others or stuff to be our god for one reason only: above all,
ME. That's the sin of pride. God's place and God's space is the
desert: the place of letting go, the place of emptiness and nothing
(no things). Who wants to be there? Nobody will see us in the
desert, so we go backwards to the world of stuff. We go back
to where we were, back to slavery, like the Israelites in Egypt,
back to the fleshpots (Exodus 16:1-13). We don't realize we have
to go through the desert if we want to get to the Promised Land.
Emptiness comes before fullness. We don't see this. We're so filled
with ourselves, that we can't see God's plan for our redemption
from slavery. Above all, ME.

The Blimp

Hovering high above big sporting events is the Goodyear Blimp.
It wants to be noticed. It wants everyone to know its name. It wants
to be seen on television.
The sin of pride is the attempt to inflate ourselves—to appear
bigger and better and higher than everyone else. Our lifetime fantasy is to be a "Goodme Blimp," floating high above the crowd,
seen by everyone and having everyone know our name. We want

everyone to see us and say, "Look, there's the Goodme Blimp." True or false? Agree or disagree? Do you do that? If you don't think you're into that fantasy game, would any of these dream titles fit you: Goodguy Blimp, Goodperson Blimp, Goodnurse Blimp, Goodsaint Blimp, Goodrich Blimp, Goodathlete Blimp, Goodstudent Blimp, Goodparent Blimp, Goodpriest Blimp, Goodpresident Blimp, Goodmechanic Blimp, Goodworker Blimp, Goodproblemperson Blimp, Goodpainintheass Blimp, Goodboy Blimp, Goodgirl Blimp, Goodguywiththegreatsportscar Blimp?
Hey world. Look at Me.

The Tower

The sin of pride has often been symbolized by a tower. The King or the Queen is up there above the rest of us. That image was dreamed up before the Blimp. Today images could be the big desk, big office, rich clothes, lots of money, expensive car, first class seats, a big title, degrees, a big house, lots of children, less children, no children, more toys, costly gadgets, a great body, etc. The list is endless on the ways and means people use to try to tower above the rest of the crowd.

We want to be up there with the gods. We want to be bright like the sun, so that people will look up to us in the day. We want to be a star, so that people will look up to us in the night. Pride is the plot of novels and movies. It makes the world go round.

Religion

If pride is everywhere, and if pride is sneaky, we should expect to find it in religion. The devil was an angel. Saints have fallen from grace. The Tower of Babel was built by people who wanted to make a name for themselves and be as high as God. Pride sneaks around religious circles in all kinds of clever disguises and vestments. Spiritual writers through the ages have always warned religious people about having a "holier than thou" attitude.

Then there are the subtle traps of trying to be the best former worst sinner in the monastery or the best humble person in the community.

If there was any one sin that Jesus the Rabbi went after, it was pride. He told us to pray, but to pray in our inner room. Moreover, close the door. Pray to your Father in private. "Don't behave like the hypocrites who love to stand and pray in synagogues or on street corners in order to be noticed" (Matthew 6:1-18). Two people went up to the local church to pray. Both were sinners, but the first one didn't know it. The first person said: "Thank god, I am not like the rest of the people in this parish—selfish, lazy and always sitting around watching R-rated video movies on their televisions or like that lady back there in the rear of the church. She looks like a bag lady with all her packages. I come to church at least five times a week. I attend all the parish functions. I always put my envelopes in the collection. And I always show up to work at bingo, unlike half the people around here. The second person knelt there in the rear of the church, unable to lift her face to the presence of her God. She kept saying inwardly, "Lord, be merciful to me a sinner."

Pride then is a sneaky sin. It's so easy to see it in others. In fact, we love to see it in others. It's so difficult to see it in ourselves. Basically, then, it's a blindness and a refusal to admit that we can't see. Everyone wants to see. Right? Everyone wants to be right. Right? And when we are wrong we want to cover up so that we will look right. Right? The New Testament uses many words to describe pride. The three best are: stubbornness, blindness and righteousness.

Crumbling Towers

Jesus warned us about being overinflated—having "I" trouble. The first are going to be last and the last are going to be first. Someday the proud tower is going to crumble and the blimp is going to run out of gas and crash. "Everyone who exalts himself

shall be humbled and he who humbles himself shall be exalted.''
Kings and presidents, popes and bishops, need to be reminded
of their origins: the earth. Don't we love people who are down
to earth? Don't we laugh at those who try to be up in the air—
especially with their nose. We all need court jesters, Shakespeare
and political cartoonists. We all need to mix with ''the common
clay'' and make mistakes: to spill coffee and to put our foot in
our mouth every once and a while.

During a car ride, an old priest quoted to me the saying, ''If
it rained miters (bishops' hats), none would hit the ground.'' Continuing, he added, ''It's got to be difficult being a bishop: having
people making a fuss over you, people flattering you, parents holding up little kids and pointing at you. It's got to go to their heads.''
John Lindsay, former mayor of New York City, once said, ''Flattery isn't harmful, unless inhaled.''

But don't we all inhale it? Don't we all eat it up? But pride is
especially dangerous for those who are already a step off the
ground: those with cute or bright children and those with several
degrees, those who have big salaries and those with big jobs, those
who have high I.Q.'s and those who can sing, those who preach
and those who teach. Those who climb the ladder of success or
the steps of the altar or go up to the head table, better be careful,
lest they lose touch with those they think they leave behind.

Then there is the danger of wanting more: more praise, more
flattery, more money, more prestige, more honors, more anything
that will put us higher than those we think beneath us. I could
never understand why people make the comment, ''Why would
anyone want to be the president, or the mayor, or the senator?
The aggravation and the traveling around would drive anyone
crazy. They could make a lot more money in private industry or
in business.''

Down deep we all know the reason why people want more and
want to make it to the top. And down deep is where we have to
look when it comes to pride. Jesus kept warning the Pharisees about
living on the surface—seeing life as a show. He told them to look

down deep. On the surface they looked like a beautiful cemetery—
nice green leaves—beautiful white stones; but underneath are dead
bones and stink. Everybody knows that.

Jesus, the Humble One

The horror of pride is that we no longer see the truth. The horror of pride is that it separates us from others. When we are up
there on the ladder of success or in the Blimp or in the Tower
or up in the pulpit or the head table, we might get dizzy because
of the heights. Mountain air can do that. And the people down
there in the valley can seem so small. There's the danger.

One day Peter, John and James climbed a mountain with Jesus.
While up there, they experienced the transfigured Jesus in all his
glory. It was like waking from a dream for these three fishermen.
They now experienced something the other disciples hadn't. They
wanted to stay up there. But like Moses in all his glory, Jesus had
to come down from the mountain and be with the people in the
valley and the plains. And on that day when they came down from
the mountain, Jesus had to warn his disciples about ambition and
who was the greatest. Were Peter, John and James still filled with
mountain air? It's hard to come down, once you've been up there.
Jesus took a little child, someone small, someone we have to look
down to, and told us, "Whoever welcomes this little child on my
account welcomes me, and whoever welcomes me welcomes him
who sent me; for the least among you is the greatest" (Luke
9:28-50).

Isn't that what God did? God emptied himself, deflated himself,
becoming a little child in our midst, ready for all those who will
accept him. "He was in the world, and through him the world
was made, yet the world did not know who he was. To his own
he came, yet his own did not accept him." Then comes the Good
News: "Any who did accept him he empowered to become children
of God" (John 1:1-18; Philippians 2:1-11).

Stable or Inn?

Do you have room in your Inn for Jesus? Luke tells us that there was no room in the Inn. It was all filled up. Then do you have any room in your Stable for Jesus? Luke tells us that is the place where Jesus is born.

The journey from the Inn to the Stable is the journey from Pride to Humility. The Pharisees and all those who are filled up with pride refuse to look within and see that their center is a Stable. Instead, they want to be seen as an Inn—but that's not where Jesus is born.

MANTRA: *"Everyone who exalts himself (herself) shall be humbled and she (he) who humbles herself (himself) shall be exalted."*

37. BECOMING UNSTUCK

PEOPLE get stuck.

Have you ever been stuck? Use your journal and write about the feelings you've experienced when you were stuck. Read your autobiography and get in touch with moments when you felt stuck. Without money? Without a job? Fired? Broken? Lost? Rejected? Betrayed? Caught? Unable to forgive? Walked out on? Filled with resentments? The other refused to talk to you? Used? Abused? Failed? Depressed? Angry? Frustrated?

Everybody knows what it's like to be stuck. We all have been caught in habits, sins, patterns, hurts, situations, jobs, relationships, places, spaces and cases that killed us.

One of the basic hopes that these meditations have been stressing over and over again is to push you to see situations in your life where you are stuck and where you can change. The plan is that while you are reading a meditation you will find yourself thinking and saying, "I have to get out of here."

The choice is always ours. A or B? Freedom or Slavery? Grace or Sin? The Right or the Left Side of the Golden Bridge? Sheep or Goat? Wheat or Weed? The Promised Land or Egypt? Stable or Inn? Unstuck or Stuck? The choice is always ours.

One of my favorite authors is Jean-Paul Sartre, the French existentialist. If there is any one message that I think about when reading his reflections, it is the challenge and the responsibility to choose what happens in my life instead of letting it happen. Act don't react. He saw so many people living lives of self-deception. One of his famous images is that of the waiter in the restaurant playing being a waiter. He has all the moves. He says all the right things. But he's putting on an act. He's playing a role. So many of us go through life stuck. We play roles. We try to say the right things. Christians mimic being a Christian. Speakers play at being speakers.

If we're stuck, should we give up thinking there is *No Exit*, that life is *Nausea*, and we are stuck in a hell hole? He would answer that there are some aspects of life that we are stuck with. We can't change our background, but we can freely choose new forms of life for our future.

The first decision is to become unstuck. And often that means becoming unglued, to fall apart. It brings on anxiety, but it can also put us on the road to freedom. And making that choice will bring social pressure, isolation and loneliness. It can also bring new freedom, new life and new passion. As Sartre often said, "Life begins on the far side of despair." No wonder people don't want to move. No wonder people prefer to remain stuck.

The Bible is also all about life. It's all about people who are stuck and decided to become unstuck. It's also about people who were challenged to change and refused to become unstuck. Exodus or No Exodus? Therefore, it's a book of hope and despair. Which pattern, which choice can you identify with: those who move or those who prefer to remain stuck in their old patterns of death?

Abraham, Moses, the prophets, were called to leave home and start a new life elsewhere. Jesus the Rabbi also left home and preached that same message over and over again. Some people listened and stayed where they were. Some people listened and changed. The choice is always ours.

Where are you?

The Prodigal Son got stuck. He made some dumb moves in his life. He found himself caught in a pig pen with nothing to eat but slop. "Life begins on the far side of despair." He hit bottom and decided to look up. He got smart and decided to become unstuck. After waking up, his first move was to admit his stupidity. You're more apt to get enlightened in a pig pen than in a church or in front of a television set. He went home to a father who was not stuck. But surprise! Who would ever have expected that the older brother became the main character in the story? Jesus put him in to try to get all those who are stuck in resentments and the inability to forgive to wake up and become unstuck. Instead of worrying about his brother, it looks like he spent all his working hours fantasizing about what his younger brother was doing—and getting angrier with every image.

Have you ever been in either brother's shoes? Have you ever made a gigantic mistake, betrayed somebody by infidelity, spent some time in the pig pen, ruined the family name, and felt like you were living in a garbage dumpster in the back of a greasy diner? Have you ever been stuck in fears that you couldn't go home and ask forgiveness and try to start all over again? Or have you ever been in the other pair of shoes? You're the one who has been hurt or left behind, stuck with taking care of old dad. Someone else ruined the family name. And you're stuck with all these feelings of anger and resentment and the inability to forgive.

Look at Peter and Judas. One denied Christ and the other betrayed Christ. Both had to live with their mistakes. One chose to hang himself; the other chose to live and be forgiven. Peter became unstuck and discovered what it is to be loved. He must have listened to the story of the Prodigal Son when Jesus told it.

Part III of this book was all about some of the basic ways people get stuck: cruelty, giving up, resenting the past, if-ing'' life away, envy, sloth, greed, gluttony, lust, anger and pride. They are some of the weeds that are stuck in our field.

The hope is that you realize that even though we are stuck with memories and mistakes, we can also remove some of the weeds in our field and learn from the other ones we can't remove. Whenever weeds are removed, we then have room for new life in our field—the themes which will be talked about in Part IV of this book.

MANTRA QUOTE: *"Life begins on the far side of despair"*
(Sartre).

PART IV
The Planting

"Jesus proposed still another parable:
The reign of God is like a mustard
seed which someone took and planted
in his field. It is the smallest seed
of all, yet when full-grown it is
the largest of plants. It becomes so
big a shrub that the birds of the
sky come and build their nests in
its branches."

(Matthew 13:31-32)

38. TWO GRAVES

I DON'T know about you, but a cemetery is the most sacred ground that I walk on—even when I don't know any person who is buried there. Here at our novitiate we have a cemetery where many from our community are buried. It's an extra special place, because some good memories are buried in my heart of those whose remains lie below.

When walking in that cemetery, two graves have the most drawing power. They are the graves of two priests who happen to be buried next to each other. They died, one right after the other.

Both were alcoholics. One didn't recover, but the other one did, thank God. I met both of them several times and experienced their presence. One man carried the look of a man always running, always looking elsewhere. One man carried the look of deep serenity and joy.

I met "X" for the first time back in 1968. It was at a clergy gettogether on the Lower East Side of New York. During the "Happy Hour" before the dinner, in walked this priest. Someone said to me, "There's Father X." His eyes searched for the table with the bottles. Over his shoulder was a blue traveling bag. He gulped down three quick drinks and shot out the door, almost as fast as he came in. Off into the night before I got a chance to say hello to him.

I met "Y" a few years later, just after he started his recovery. I heard his A.A. story. What a great conversion. "Y" radiated hope and joy. People connected with him easily, especially, I think, because of a great smile. Understanding was his gift. He had been there.

Both had painful deaths. Y died of cancer—with friends. X died alone in a boarding house away from our community. His body wasn't discovered for a few days. He would often disappear for a while, always refusing help.

Alcoholism hits almost every family and community. So, too, death. We have all been to funerals and cemeteries, and I suppose what causes the most grief are the stories that have an unhappy ending. We go through life with the hope that those with problems will come back to life before they die. We all pray that X, Y and Z will recover.

St. Alphonsus, the one who founded the Redemptorists, the community I belong to, wrote a book, *Preparation for Death*. Its purpose is the same as the talk on "The Four Last Things: Death, Judgment, Heaven or Hell" on a Redemptorist Parish Mission. And that purpose was to scare the hell out of people, to wake people up to life, instead of death, during life.

Some of the book is out of date, but obviously death can never be out of date. Neither can meditation on it. St. Alphonsus' basic message on all this was: Remember death and you'd live a good life (Sirach 28:6). He said, "How clearly are the truths of faith seen at the hour of death."

Why not stop to see them clearly now. And one good way is

to do what Alphonsus keeps suggesting in his book and in his sermons: picture your family and friends standing at your grave. What will they feel and what will they remember?

Isn't that a great question to meditate upon? I'm sure you feel my sadness standing at X's grave and my joy standing at Y's grave. To be honest, because the graves are next to each other, the sadness overwhelms the joy.

Don't we stand before the grave of a person we know and say three of four things:

1) Death: "He or she is dead."
2) Judgment: "What was their life like?"
3) Heaven: "It was a pleasure to know her or him."
4) Hell: "They were hell to live with."

What is your judgment on yourself right now? Do people see you alive or dead? Are you a pleasure to be with or do you cause hell? What is God's judgment on you?

Part III of this book talked about sin and hell and some of those things that make life miserable, the things that need to be uprooted from our field.

Part IV, obviously, will talk about heaven—the Kingdom of Heaven—the planting of some things in our field that make life a joy for those we are with.

Heaven or hell? The choice is always ours.

X didn't reach out for help. Y realized he couldn't do it alone and asked for help. What about you?

Have you found out yet that you can't do it alone? What about those people who will be standing over your grave? Can any of them help you? What about the priest who blessed your coffin? What about Jesus who was called upon in prayer?

"It's a Wonderful Life."

Maybe we have to die to find out how to live.

"It's a Wonderful Life" was a great movie. Picture yourself

as the main character. Imagine family and friends above your grave talking about you.

What was your life like?

MANTRA QUESTION: *"X or Y, what will it be?"*

39. THE GNAWING

GNAWING beneath the ground, groping in the dark, down deep in the great unvisited spaces of our heart, there is an itch, a biting claw, a hunger, a desire for what isn't, a need, a hope for what we don't have. We know down deep that the life we are living now is not enough.

God gnaws at us. God rides buses and planes with us; however it's usually when we are alone. We look out the bus or plane window from inside ourselves and things outside look different. Something's missing. We know there has to be more.

God visits us at night, in the dark when we can't sleep, in the hospital or after going to a wake, after a fight or the "wrong" phone call.

God knocks on our cellar door in the depths of hurt. Or, surprise—God comes in joyful moments. There is God on the edge of the crowd when everything is music and dance, and in the height of ecstasy, we know down deep there is a missing.

God is in these feelings of emptiness, in the desert, in the blank spaces, in the nothingness, in the hunger and thirst for completeness. Karl Rahner, in his book *Encounters with Silence,* asks God these questions:

"Why do you torment me with your infinity, if I can never really measure it?"

"Why do you constrain me to walk along your paths, if they lead only to the awful darkness of your night, where only you can see?"

"Why have you burnt your mark in my soul in Baptism?"

"Why have you kindled in me the flame of faith, this dark light which lures us out of the bright security of our little huts into your night?"

We know some answers. We know how things grow. First there

ıs the seed, then there is the pumpkin. And we know that we would rather be the pumpkin, or the flower, or the wheat, and not go through all these struggles involved in growth.

Jesus the Rabbi taught us that's the way we have to go. There are no short cuts. "I solemnly assure you, unless the grain of wheat falls to the earth and dies, it remains just a grain of wheat. But if it dies, it produces much fruit. The person who loves his life in this world preserves it to life eternal" (John 12:24-25).

Who wants to die? We'd rather stay on the surface and think that's life. In the meanwhile, deep below the surface the dream for a better life gnaws at us.

Seeds down deep don't get the glory. Flowers, wheat, the pumpkins get all the notices. Some pumpkins even win contests. Some flowers and wheat make it to the altar. And so we choose surface living. We want results. We want the finished product. We pick and wear flowers, but never the roots.

There are two levels: the seed below the top soil and the pumpkin above the ground. The choice is always ours. Choose the seed and you'll also get the pumpkin—in time—but you'll have to die. Choose the pumpkin and you'll be bought.

Years ago I saw a poster that got me thinking. I ended up using it in many sermons, because it made so much sense to me. A sweating, big, fat guy was leaning against a refrigerator door with his hand ready to open it. Beneath the picture were the words, "Inside every fat person, there is a thin person dying to get out."

Isn't that the inside story on all of us. We want what isn't. But we know we have to die to get it.

Inside every angry person, there's a patient person dying to get out.

Inside every sinner, there's a saint dying to get out.

Inside every person that has given up on religion and churches, there's a person who hungers for a God and a religion that is real, where prayer is prayer, and a religious service is a religious experience.

Inside every child, there's an adult trying to get out. (Watch little children imitate the big ones.)

Inside every lonely person, there is an outgoing person dying to break out.

Haven't you met an authentic holy person somewhere in your life, and you began to feel inner longings to become holy yourself?

Haven't you seen someone jogging or in great shape, and you said to yourself, "I've got to get moving again?"

Haven't you thought about Jesus having powerful religious experiences in the desert and on the mountains and then seen him come down into the temple and explode in anger because of the buyers and sellers and the moneychangers? Inside every church and temple is a holy place wanting to be discovered.

Haven't you experienced Jesus in special moments in your life, where his words were different than all the television or coffee break words, different from the gossip and the whisperings? In that moment didn't you know down deep, in the soil of your being, in the great unvisited spaces of your heart, that He is the one who has the words of eternal life?

Haven't you experienced being fed up with the selfishness and stupidity, greed and fighting and you knew there had to be something better in life? Haven't you felt words like these from D. H. Lawrence: "Men and women aren't really dogs: they only look like it and behave like it. Somewhere inside there is a great chagrin and a gnawing discontent?"

Haven't you always known what Jesus meant when he said, "The Kingdom of God is within?"

MANTRA PRAYER: *"Deep down God,*
speak to me;
deep down God,
help me to listen to you."

40. WE'RE IT

ONCE, while visiting a group of religious sisters, I was asked to say Mass, sort of on the spot, like five minutes from now and I said, "Yes."

In the sacristy, while putting on the Mass vestments, I looked at the scripture reading for the day. Reading to myself, I said, "Oh no!" It was the saying of Jesus, "Whenever you give a lunch or dinner, do not invite your friends or brothers or relatives or wealthy neighbors. They might invite you in return and thus repay you. No, when you have a reception, invite beggars and the crippled, the lame and the blind. You should be pleased that they cannot repay you, for you will be repaid in the resurrection of the just" (Luke 14:12-14).

Now if there is any one message of Jesus that makes me feel guilty, it's those words. I've always had food to eat. And never once in my life have I invited to dinner beggars, the crippled, the lame and the blind.

I know of parishes and centers that have soup kitchens, but that's not the rectory dining room or individual homes. Jesus' words, then, about inviting the beggars, the crippled, the lame and the blind, have always been an invitation for me to feel guilty.

I do remember feeding men who came in from the road or the streets. I sat down with them and both of us ate what I put together. However, we ate at the kitchen table. It was never an invitation to our community meal. If I had a home of my own, would I? Fantasy says "yes"; but the odds say "no."

It was time to go out to say Mass. My five minutes were up. I stood there in the sacristy before going out to the chapel. "To preach or not to preach?" I decided not to. Who wants to hear unprepared words? Who wants to eat an uncooked meal?

After I read the Gospel, I was all prepared to sit down for a few minutes of quiet reflection instead of a homily. Inwardly, however, I heard the words, "You're it."

And without knowing it, there I was preaching a short homily.

"As Christians, we religious probably feel guilty everytime we hear this Gospel. At least I know I do. I don't remember ever in my whole life inviting beggars to our dinner table. I've never heard a confrere say to me before supper, 'Guess who's coming to dinner?' and then tell me he invited three people from the Bowery for supper.

"But guess what? We're it. We are the beggars, the crippled, the lame and the blind. And Jesus has invited us to this meal—to this banquet, to this community.

"We're poor beggars. We're so blind that we walk by each other every day, without noticing that each of us is in need. We are so deaf, we don't hear those we live with. We use the television, so we can be with each other, but not listen to each other. We're so lame and crippled that we don't walk with each other, nor do we walk up the stairs to each other's room to see how the other is doing.

"We're it!"

I sat down after my short homily for a few minutes reflection. After Mass nobody said anything about the homily.

Driving home that evening, I turned off the car radio, even though I was listening to a New York Knicks basketball game. (They were doing better then.) I found myself thinking about my homily. Was I copping out? Of course, I was. We still don't invite to our community table the beggars, the crippled, the lame and the blind.

"You're it!"

I heard the words again. I began thinking. For twenty-six years as a religious and twenty-one years as a priest I never really worked for or with the very poor. Moreover, our community was founded to work for "the poorest and most abandoned souls." That always compounded my guilt. As a Christian and as a Redemptorist I was supposed to be working with the poor.

During my two years in an inner city parish, I spent a lot of time visiting with shut-ins—often sharing their tea. That took away some of my guilt feelings. In retreat work for fourteen years, I tried to be available for anyone and everyone. We ate all our meals with the retreatants. Most were middle-class and they paid for their retreat. So there was no actual work with beggars, the crippled, the blind and the lame.

Several times I read commentaries about Jesus' words. I could say it's an allegory. I could say it's all about the Early Church and that many of its members were the poor beggars, the crippled, the blind and the lame, or that the Early Church was urging its members to help the poor by presenting a high ideal! I could say the words were about the Eucharist.

But that was then, what about today? I drove home that night still wondering.

"You're it!"

I laughed. There it was again. I am it. What I want as a Christian and a religious is to be rich in spiritual bragging rights: "I work with the poor." "I am out there with the poorest of the poor." "I am part of a community that has no barriers. Our homes are open to all—especially the poor. All come to our dinner table."

I have always envied Dorothy Day and the Catholic Workers homes where the poor and some of the Catholic Workers live together.

"You're it!"

We don't do that. That's a part of our poverty. And we probably never will do it. As a result we don't have bragging rights that our community invite the poor to eat with us. And young people who join us will be disappointed because they have high ideals. Some will be disappointed and some will leave, and hopefully some will move us closer to the ideal.

Yes, some of our men work with the poorest of the poor. But I'll probably go through life feeling guilty that I've never really been with the poorest of the poor. That's poverty. I'll always feel guilty. And I'll always feel guilty when I hear Jesus' words to invite the beggars, not your friends, to your table and we'll probably continue to invite just our friends.

And after I die, if the Lord says to me, "I was hungry and you gave me no food, I was thirsty and you gave me no drink, I was away from home and you gave me no welcome, naked and you gave me no clothing, I was ill and in prison and you did not come to comfort me" (Matthew 25:42-43), I will not say, "Lord when did I see you hungry, and thirsty and naked?" I'll remain silent in my guilt and my poverty. But if I'm sent to hell for not feeding the poor, I say to Jesus, "Practice what you preach. Here I am a poor beggar, begging for food in the eternal banquet. I was blind and lame and a cripple all my life. Don't just invite your friends to your table. Invite me the beggar, the poor man and the stranger.

You're it, Jesus. And if you send me to hell, I'll try to make you feel so guilty, that you'll have to invite us sinners to your table.

MANTRA: *"The poor you always have with you"*
(John 12:8).

41. CENTERING

ONE of my mom's favorite sayings is, "The moo is out of me." She uses it when she's playing cards. It's her way of saying, "That's enough. I'm tired. I need a break." I notice she says it more often when she's losing than when she's winning.

When she's winning, when she's really in her game, all her energies are on the cards. She knows which cards have been played and which ones are still out.

Me? When I play cards, I also like to win. But I rarely put all my energies into the game. Fifty-two cards are too many to keep track of. My center is elsewhere, especially when I'm losing.

What about you? Are you good at cards? Can you center all your energies into what you're doing? Or do you tend to switch channels and go elsewhere?

"Where your treasure is, there's your heart."

Jesus the Rabbi said that he noticed that everybody is a searcher, a channel switcher, looking for the best program, searching for the treasure of our life. That's what we put all our time, money and energies into.

Hopefully, we'll find or have found the treasure, the Kingdom, the answer that we can center our life on. Jesus said, "The Kingdom of God is like a buried treasure which someone found in a field. They hid it again, and rejoicing at their find went and sold all that they had and bought that field. Or again, the Kingdom of Heaven is like a merchant's search for fine pearls. When he found one really valuable pearl, he went back and put up for sale all that he had bought it" (Matthew 13:44-46).

Now that's centering. Where is your center? What do you "moo" for? That cow wants help. What do you want?

When I'm giving a talk, and it's starting to get too long when I sense the "moo" is out of everyone, I often say, "Where is everybody?" If it's time to stop the "game," I'll call it quits. I learned that from playing cards. I've sat in enough classrooms,

heard enough lectures, been on enough retreats, given enough talks
to know we're often not where our bodies are.

Where are you right now? Have I lost you? Is the "moo" out
of you? Should I have shut up a long time ago? Have I said anything
that touched your center?

Fifty-two meditations are a lot of meditations to juggle. As I
said, when I play cards, fifty-two cards are too many cards to keep
track of. As I was writing this book, I often had to put my pen
down and go elsewhere to have my energies restored. I also had
to backcheck on what I've said so far, and ask where am I headed.

This book has evolved as the year went along. It began with
the request from The Thomas More Association to put together
fifty-two meditations for the fifty-two weeks of the year. That
sounded possible, so I agreed to do it.

Where am I now? Where are you now? Have I said things that
touched your core, your center? What's on your mind? What's
central? Who's at your center? Is there anything that I can say
before the end of this book to help you, to encourage you, to challenge you? What should I center on? These are the questions I'm
asking myself right now. What questions are you asking?

With regards to this specific meditation on centering I was
wondering just what to say. Lots of images and examples came
to mind. Then it hit me that I needed to center in on the process
of this book. To me that would be a good example of what centering is all about. We pull over to the side of the road and stop
the car. We get out the map to see where we're going and where
we came from.

The main theme of this book on spirituality centers around
conversion—the call to make significant changes in my life. The
main person whom I have presented as advocating and teaching
conversion is Jesus the Rabbi. The main image is the individual
as a field.

Part I talked about conversion. Part II talked about some helps
in the conversion process. Part III presented what needed to be
changed and uprooted: the weeds, the sins, in our field. Part IV

is beginning to talk about the wheat—the good things that need to be planted in our field.

Part IV began with the constant stress of this book: "The choice is always ours." Look at the end of your life. Stand at your grave. Would you rather be X or Y? Then I talked about God's presence in our life as the gnawing beneath the surface of the field. Life is a hunger and a thirst for more—and that more is God. Next I wanted to point out a very important assumption that I have. Down deep we're poor. We would love to be rich in holiness, but we're poor. And surprise, that makes us the kind of people that Jesus loves.

This meditation is on centering—because I wanted to ask you where your focus is. It's important to know what your core is. It's important to know what's drawing you. It's important to know whether you're divided.

Notice how often people drop things, bang cars, make mistakes, hurt themselves, because they are leading double lives, because their mind is elsewhere.

Isn't that what Jesus said? "No servant can serve two masters. Either he will hate the one and love the other or be attentive to the one and despise the other" (Luke 16:13).

What's drawing you? Is it you? Or is there a backseat driver?

Till we become centered, till we make the decision for the right single vision, we'll never really be happy.

Division, especially long division, can kill us.

Look at your field. Look at the rest of your life. What do you want for it? What do you want growing there? How can you be a better servant towards the people in your field?

Seeing those questions as central, I want to present the remaining meditations of this book as reflections on that question. The next meditation will present Jesus as the Lord and Center of life. Up until now the main stress has been on Jesus as Rabbi. After this meditation I'm going to reflect on the following issues:

—Learning patience and how to wait

—Being a giving person
—Saying "I love you"
—Saying "Thank you"
—Saying "I forgive you"
—Dealing with suffering
—Living life to the full
—Not counting the cost
—Growth in the spirit
—Seeing my connections with others

Then the "moo" will be out of me and I'll end this book.

MANTRA: *"Where your treasure is, there your heart is also."*

42. JESUS IS LORD

IN the early pages of this book I mentioned my rediscovery in the past two years of Jesus as Rabbi. And throughout this book I have described Jesus as a Rabbi who has given provocative teachings—words that would challenge people who wanted to live a better life.

To anyone who has dropped out of Church because of boredom, poor services, hurt, loss of faith, laziness, etc., I would strongly suggest: Approach Jesus as a Rabbi. Reflect on his sayings and parables. Go from Chapters 10 to 20 in Luke or the Sermon on the Mount, Chapters 5 to 7 in Matthew.

Everyone can relate to the gift of meeting a good teacher, whether it was Miss Smith in the fourth grade or an ethics professor at the University of Maryland. We all have read something in Dear Abby or in *Reader's Digest* that made an awful lot of sense. Then there are the writers from the past whose wisdom is challenging to us today, whether it's Augustine or Pascal, Isaiah or Plato, Meister Eckhart or Kierkegaard.

But none of those teachers are perceived as Jesus is perceived. We might have said of a high school English teacher, "We worshipped the ground she walked on." And even if she worked "miracles" in the classroom, we were not ready to go to her house on Sunday morning to worship her. We are with Jesus if we perceive him as God. There is a great distance between Rabbi and God. I think stating that distinction is very helpful for what I have been saying in this book about Jesus and what I want to say now.

On New Year's Eve, a bit after midnight, right after 1959 changed to 1960, I experienced Jesus in a new way. The experience was Presence. Till then I believed that Jesus was God and also human. I was a baptized Christian. I prayed, went to Church, never doubted my Catholic traditions, and all that. I believed Jesus rose from the dead and was present in the bread and wine of the Mass, and in the people as the Body of Christ. The place was Ilchester,

Maryland. I was a novice preparing to take first vows in our community. After the new year came in, I went to our chapel to say a short prayer before going to bed. All was dark—all was quiet—except for a candle in the sanctuary. As I sat there in the silence, I experienced Jesus in a new way for me. All those who have met Jesus—or another person in a lifetime relationship—know you can't put what happened into words. It's just one person being in the real presence of another person and both knowing they are in each other's presence.

It was before the Charismatic movement came to the Catholic Church. At the time, Catholics wouldn't think of having a bumper sticker: "Jesus is Lord." It was before the Ecumenical Movement and dialogue with Protestants. Karl Barth and other Protestant theologians wondered why Catholics at times seemed to bypass Jesus and apply feelings and terms for Jesus to the Pope or others. For example, Barth said that the words, "I am the Good Shepherd" were applied to St. Peter, the Pope or the Church, but after all, Jesus was the one who said the words of himself in the first place.

Yes, Catholics apply those words to St. Peter, the Pope and the Church. It doesn't mean, however, that we drop Jesus. Being a Catholic and having a Pope evoke great feelings and meanings for us—even if we have disagreements with the Pope or with aspects of the Church. However, it seems that non-Catholics misunderstand what Catholics understand about the Pope and the Catholic Church. You have to be a Catholic to get a feel for our feelings about the Pope and our Church. Fourteen years of retreat work taught me that Catholics love their Church. And love means you know the things you like and don't like and still love. Catholics have lots of gripes and lots of suggestions, some for the Pope, but most for their local priests and Church. I, too, would love to see lots of "fluff stuff" go, along with the way things seem to operate at times, but I'll live and die a Catholic. Watch a Catholic's eyes and body language when he hears the Pope is coming to town. And if they see the Pope in person they will remember the time, place, and date for the rest of their life—just as I remember the moment and place of a deep experience with Jesus: Ilchester, Maryland, January 1, 1960, 12:30 a.m. I can still picture a moment in St. Peter's Square, May 30, 1984, standing behind Bill Walton, the basketball player, hoping to shake the Pope's hand. Neither of us did, but I'll never forget that day.

So our experience and love of the Pope and our Church does not block our experience and love of Jesus. When they do, somebody will speak out. St. Alphonsus, who started the religious congregation that I belong to, wrote over a hundred books. Some criticized the Church and religious practices in the Kingdom of Naples in 18th Century Europe, but over and over his main message was "the practice of the love of Jesus Christ." Non-Catholics have criticized us at times for our externals—doing the very thing they criticize: looking only at our externals.

The heart of the matter is what St. Alphonsus and other Catholic spiritual writers have always stressed: Jesus is Lord. The message has appeared in different external words and forms, but Jesus as Lord has always been the central theme of Catholicism.

I knew all that. What happened to me on that New Year's Eve was a new experience of that love of Jesus. It was personal—one to one—a moment that began a bed-rock experience for my life. Once you have experienced someone, no one can tell you that you didn't. It was a gift, a grace given to me at the age of 20. I met someone who was alive 2000 years ago. I experienced the Resurrection—Easter—just after midnight, January 1, 1960. Nothing visible happened, but when religion shifts from belief in a teaching to a one-to-one encounter with a person, then an earthquake can happen within.

Years later I read about similar moments of experiencing the personal God in books like *Mysticism* by Evelyn Underhill and *The Varieties of Religious Experience* by William James. Teresa of Avila experienced spiritual storms and rapture. Pascal experienced fire. The absolute and the infinite, are experienced in finite and immediate experience.

Jesus is Lord.

Last month, I was talking to a classmate of mine, with whom
I went through the novitiate. Unfortunately, it wasn't until then
that both of us told each other about our faith experiences. One
Sunday, while in college, as he was in church waiting for Mass
to begin, it hit him, suddenly, that Jesus is present in the Eucharist.
That moment was the beginning of changes in his life that eventually led him to enter the seminary to become a priest. It takes
us Catholics a long time to express out loud to each other: Jesus
is Lord!

The "vision" sustained me through the rest of the novitiate and
all through the six years of our major seminary. It didn't go away.
Jesus was alive. I sensed his presence every day.

After I began working as a priest, I began to experience that
same Jesus, who was present in the Blessed Sacrament, present
in the people I was visiting in the parish. What a gift, what a bless-
ing, to enter deeply into the life of people and discover God. Here
I was, a middle-class kid from Brooklyn, enjoying my work—
meeting Christ in his creations.

For example, while in Most Holy Redeemer Parish—East Third
Street, on the Lower East Side of New York—I met Annie and
Willie Williams. Once both of them were in the hospital at the
same time. However, Annie was in Beth Israel and Willie at
Belleview. I would visit Willie and tell him what Annie had told
me about her the day before. Then I would go down to Annie and
tell her the love words he wanted me to bring her from him. It's
quite an experience for an unmarried, twenty-seven-year-old priest,
to be in the middle of a love affair that had lasted for over fifty
years of marriage between a black man and white woman. In those
moments of love I experienced love. I knew in a new way what
the letter of John meant when it says, "God is love and the person who abides in love, abides in God and God in that person"
(1 John 4:16).

As time moved on, there were many more moments like that
as a priest—while hearing confessions, in listening to people, helping people, etc. The main surprise was that it can't be planned.

God is a God of surprise moments.

I understood Chesterton's remark, "Men (and women) are the million masks of God."

Have you experienced God?

Lots of people—including myself—have experienced God in rivers, lakes and especially the ocean. Looking up into the night sky, seeing a new-born baby, autumn leaves, eating fresh bread, being at a wedding, etc. have often brought the feeling of God's Presence. In those moments we can begin to switch from what John Henry Newman calls notional assent to real assent. We had a notion about God's existence. We said the words—the creed. Now we know for real there is a God. However, Newman would warn us about sentiment in such religious experiences. Bernard Lonergan would warn about being "foggy." The proof is in the pudding. Does the experience of God lead to conversion of life? Talk about God is cheap. The change in one's behavior to a greater service of neighbor is the first test of a true conversion. Don't talk about giving me an apple! Work the ground. Plant a tree. Care for it. Then hand me from the fruit of your tree. "By their fruits you shall know them."

What about knowing Jesus?

When my brother died, one of the most lonely feelings was being in the presence of someone who didn't know him, who had never experienced the most interesting person I ever met. If you didn't know him, you didn't feel what I was feeling. Without planning it, I said at the end of my homily at his funeral, "Thanks for knowing Pat." The church was filled with people who knew him. Wow, did that help! And when I said that last line, I sensed joy and support from those who knew him and also a loneliness in me, because some of the persons present only heard of him and had never met him.

Isn't that what the opening paragraph of the First Letter of John is saying? We're writing to you about someone we have met, someone whom we have touched, someone whom we enjoyed, and our joy won't be complete till you have that same experience. That basic dynamic is what propelled thousands of early followers of Jesus to proclaim his name throughout the Middle East.

Have you experienced Jesus yet? The second test is the need to tell others about him. The test is that you feel loneliness in the presence of those who have not experienced him yet.

MANTRA: *"Jesus is Lord!"*

43. WAITING: TWENTY QUESTIONS

THE following are twenty questions for the next time you're looking for something to do while you are waiting.

1) Can women wait better than men? Babies take nine months
to be born; planting the seed is much quicker.

2) Are farmers more patient than city folks? Do they find it easier
to wait at banks and loan agencies? Waiting for seeds to grow and
bud takes time, but so too does waiting for subways, buses, traffic, etc.

3) Is this generation more impatient than earlier generations? Do
instant cereal, instant coffee, instant replay, microwave ovens,
cable TV, video movies, instant copy machines, instant read-outs
from computers, prevent people from learning how to wait?

4) Do couples without children miss out by not waiting up at night
with a sick child, waiting for kids to grow, waiting for kids to
come home safely from camp or the movies?

5) If you are or if you were a waiter or a waitress in a restaurant,
what would be the three most important things you would do to
give good service to your customers?

6) If you broke your leg and had to sit around healing from four
to six weeks, what would you do with your time? Would it be
a joyful break (pardon the pun) or would you "go bananas," not
knowing what to do with your time?

7) Still in the broken leg situation, what five books are you looking
for time to read?

8) You are sitting waiting in a doctor's waiting room and in walk the following three people: a teen-age girl on crutches, her foot in a cast; a woman who seems to be seven months pregnant; and an old lady in her seventies. Which of the three would you most likely give your seat to?

9) Or you're in the same waiting room, but this time standing with those same three people. Seated is an eighteen-year-old boy, obviously into body building. Would you suggest to him that he offer his seat to one of the three persons?

10) Do you usually keep people waiting? Or are you usually on time? If you're often late, do you do it to all people in all kinds of situations or is it usually to one person or one situation?

11) Do you answer mail or phone calls immediately, or are you a procrastinator, putting people off for hours, days and weeks?

12) When you pray, do you get restless? What's your patience level? Do you get restless after ten, twenty, forty, or sixty minutes? What are your feelings about Jesus' words, "Could you not watch with me for one hour?"

13) Why did Jesus wait till he was around thirty before he started moving around as a preacher?

14) Why did Jesus curse the fig tree in Matthew and not give it a second chance, while in Luke he gives it another year? Which is the real Jesus: the Jesus of Matthew or Luke?

15) Is there someone who is waiting for you to say to them, "I'm sorry for hurting you?"

16) Is there somebody you're waiting to come to you and prove that they are sorry for hurting you?

17) Do you cheat, when you can, on waiting in lines, trying to get ahead of others, in restaurants, at the shopping center, etc.? Do you believe in the principle of "first come, first serve"?

18) If you had cancer, would you be able to deal with all the waiting that is often involved: waiting to take tests, for the test reports, for good news? Would you be able to deal with losing hair, strength, movement?

19) You are in a barber shop or the hair dresser's. You walk in without an appointment. Four persons are ahead of you. Would you be the type that would sit and wait, or would you leave and come back another time?

20) Looking at your life, what are the three most important things you are waiting for?

MANTRA: *"Lord, teach me to learn to wait for what's worth waiting for."*

44. A GIVER OR A TAKER?

"WHEN it comes down to it, there are two kinds of people: the givers and the takers."

I retain that line from the most powerful "sermon" I ever heard. We were in a restaurant and three tables away a husband started screaming at his wife. "You're a taker. All you do is take, take, take. You never give. There are two kinds of people in the world: the givers and the takers. And God dammit, I had to marry a taker."

Everybody in the restaurant froze including the man's wife. Like everyone else, I was nervous—as if the restaurant was being held up. It was a painful sermon, as well as the one I remember the most. I can still hear all the words.

Are they still married? Was he right? Why did they marry each other? Was he a taker? Would he like to be yelled at in a restaurant?

We have all heard marriage described as a give and take situation. We've also heard the joke, "I give and he takes." We also have heard sad stories about marriages that broke apart because one or both were selfish and unwilling to give. We all have heard numbers recommended: "Marriage is a 50-50 situation." "Marriage calls for both partners giving 100 percent." "Sometimes one will give 75 percent and the other 25 percent, but if it's always the same person giving the 25 percent or the 75 percent, be aware that problems are brewing."

Are you a giver or a taker? Tha mantra at the end of this meditation is going to be simply: "Give and take." Say that a few thousand times this week and you'll begin to see yourself in a new light in all kinds of situations that you'll find yourself in.

The Giver

The giver listens. She is aware of the other person. The giver

185

"gives a damn." The giver gives it his best shot. The giver "gives till it hurts."

My dad was a giver. On Sunday afternoons when we were kids, he took us to Bliss Park in Bay Ridge, Brooklyn. Today it's a mess because of vandalism; then it was a great spot, along with its beautiful view of New York Harbor. My dad was giving my mom a break. Or he would take us to see club football games at two fields along the Belt Parkway—one at 72nd Street, the other at 96th Street, Brooklyn.

Jesus was a giver. When interrupted in prayer, because people were looking for him, he went to them. When the disciples wanted to get rid of the crowd after a long day with them, Jesus said, "Let's give them something to eat." When the little kids were trying to get to Jesus, the disciples were trying to get rid of them. Jesus said, "Let the kids come to me."

The Takers

The taker takes. She goes on long coffee breaks that take a lot of time away from work and others get stuck. He takes advantage of others. They take over the conversation. They take the best seat in the house. They take us every time and we respond, "I've been had!"

The angry man in the restaurant thought his wife was a taker. Was she? Was he projecting? We'll never know. When a marriage is breaking up, we've all heard people say, "Get a good lawyer and take your spouse for all you can get." Maybe she was doing that all through their marriage and that's why he wanted a divorce. Your move.

Giving and Taking

Jesus, at the Last Supper, gave us his body. He put in words what he had been doing all along—giving himself to all those he met—to all those who interrupted his life. And then he took a piece of bread and said, "Take and eat. This is my body which I'm giving to you."

That's the Gospel message kneaded together into the size of a piece of bread. How do we love? Answer: we give. In fact, the word "love," as we have heard so often, is overworked. It is used for everything, from selling disposable diapers to selling compact cars. I think, two other words that also end in "ve" bring out the Gospel message of love better: to gi*ve* and to ser*ve*.

A movie actor, who made it to the top, once said something like this, "When you make it to the top, make sure you think of those at the bottom. Don't just get out of the elevator, send it back down to the bottom." In other words, when you have received, make sure you give. "Cast your bread upon the waters; after a long time you may find it again" (Ecclesiastes 10:1).

Take the question of what is happening to the tropical forests of our world. They are mainly in the underdeveloped nations. Destroy them for "now" profits, and we take away from future generations. Take now and somebody will pay later. Burn forests to clear land, and the world's climate is affected because of the "greenhouse effect." Those who are cutting down hardwood trees are eliminating that industry for future generations. For example, the Brazilian rosewood is close to extinction. Drugs, fruits, nuts, spices, fragrances, as well as important insects in the life chain, are being destroyed. And often it is companies from the richer nations who are in there harvesting profits for today without thought for tomorrow.

The Ability to Receive

Some people who are good at giving are poor at taking. The secret then, is a blending of both giving and taking. Look at nature. If we take from the earth, we also have to give back to the earth. If we cut down trees, we need also to plant new ones. Nature gives many examples of this need for a blending of giving and taking. As the bees take, they are also giving.

But when it comes to people, we have all the problems. Have you ever met someone who couldn't take a break, who couldn't receive a compliment, who couldn't take a gift from you? Some people don't mind passing the salt or the strawberry jam, but cannot ask for it for themselves. Instead, they stand up and reach for it. Just as the world became a mess when there is too much taking, so too, when there is too much giving. If all were giving, who would be around to receive all these gifts? The poor resent those who only give, who never sit down to receive in return.

Here I am Lord! Jesus is a good model of someone who knew how to both give and take. He let Peter's mother-in-law make lunch for him. Mary washed his feet and dried them with her hair. Do you find it difficult letting people wait on you? Are you like Peter who wouldn't let Jesus wash his feet?

Life then is give and take. Take the Gospel in your hand and give it some thought and prayer.

MANTRA: *"Give and take."*

45. I LOVE YOU

ARE the words, "I love you" reserved only for male-female, husband-wife, very-close-friend to very-close-friend relationships?

I've noticed that many people hesitate using those three words, even people whom I would expect would say them on a regular basis.

I know, certain people spin "I love you's" all over the place and they come off as throw-away words, not meaning very much. What I'm talking about here is "I love you." If you know what I mean, you know what I mean; if you don't, you don't.

For example, I've overheard fathers and mothers unable to say to their adult chidren, "I love you." I've noticed that many long distance calls don't end with "I miss you. I love you." Adult brothers don't say to adult brothers, "I love you."

The grandchildren can do it. But adult to adult, it's often said in symbolic forms, "Take it easy now." "Drive carefully." "I hope everything will be OK." "Take care now."

Sometimes it almost comes out. It almost makes it. For example, letters end with, "Love" or "Love you" or "Love ya." Two out of the three words aren't bad.

I remember hearing a story once. I could be mixing it up, but I think it went something like this. Sammy Davis Jr. was on a TV talk show and was asked why he always says to people, "I love you." And he answered with magnum force. "Because I had a good friend once who died suddenly in an accident and I never told him, "I love you."

One of the novices here lost his brother years ago in a car accident. When my brother was dying, he said to me, "Make sure you tell your brother that you love him before he dies I didn't get that chance."

I told him that I had—not enough—but I had said it a few times. I'm learning. At first, I found it difficult. Once during a phone call, I said to myself, "Stupid, tell him!" After that it became easier to say to him, "I love you!"

We talked in person for a few days in February and we both said, "I love you" to each other when we said, "good-bye."

On Monday, March 17th, I called him in the hospital. His brain was getting too bloated with swelling, so they decided on a brain operation. He didn't sound good, so we didn't talk that long. In fact, he ended the conversation before I could say, "I love you." However, he ended his conversation exactly as follows, "Here's Joanne, I love you."

Those were his last words to me. What a beautiful gift. He had brain surgery the next day and never spoke again. I finally got down to see him that Thursday and he died the next night, March 21st.

How many people can say that the last words their brother said to them were, "I love you."

Since then I have found myself saying to people much more than I ever did in the past, "I love you." And surprise, sometimes people get up enough courage to say them in return.

Where are you with those three words? Yes, they can be said as throw-away words at the end of a get together. They can be as meaningless as an opening, "How are you?"

I love you.

Do you understand what I'm trying to say in this meditation? If you do, you know what I mean. If you don't, you don't.

MANTRA: *"I love you."*

46. "THANK YOU"

ON the car radio I once heard a Hindu Swami say something like this: "Don't get trapped into wanting to hear 'Thank you's,' because if you do, then when you don't hear 'Thank you's,' your ego will start yelling for them and get in the way. The secret is to empty the ego, to say to it, 'e - go'!"

Buddhists would give that same basic message. Be careful of desires, because they are the cause of suffering. If you desire to hear "Thank you's," you'll end up feeling hurt, because people don't always say, "Thank you."

In a way, I think, Christ is different. Once, when he healed ten people who had leprosy, he seemed hurt when only one came back to say, "Thank you." "Were not all ten made whole? Where are the other nine? Was there no one to return and give thanks to God except this foreigner?" Some would not say this: I think that our God is hurt, disappointed, or whatever word one wants to use, when we don't say, "Thank you."

Don't we all expect to hear, "Thank you's"? One of the words that is used to label the Mass is "Eucharist." It's from the Greek word for "thanks." Isn't that basically why we go to Mass: to give thanks to the Lord? I can't picture a personal God who would be indifferent to my muttering prayers of gratitude. I can't picture a God who would say, "I have no need of your thanks." One of the Preface prayers that is used at Mass has God saying that, but I find it difficult to say it.

Of course, I am projecting my human feelings onto God and a relationship with him. The Bible does it all the time. Don't we all want to hear, "Thank you," and when we don't, we feel disappointed. I expect Hindus and Buddhists to be the same.

The Man Who Never Said "Thank You."

A priest told me that he was stationed with another priest for six years, and never once did he hear him say, "Thank you."

Inwardly, he found himself dubbing him, "The Man Who Never Said, 'Thank you.'"

Philadelphia Story

Once I was preaching in Philadelphia. After Mass a lady came up to me and said, "That was a really nice sermon." And I said, "Thank you." I should have stopped there, but probably because I find it hard to receive a compliment, I added, "What did I say?" If she couldn't remember, then I would be sure that I didn't deserve the compliment. Weird? Right, but I have found myself doing that number on myself several times.

Sure enough, she said, "A...a...a...a..., but it was a good sermon."

Now she was obviously embarrassed, so to cut off her nervousness and to try to restore the situation, I asked another question, "What was the best sermon that you ever heard?"

She smiled and relaxed. "Oh, that's easy to answer. Thirteen years ago there was a Franciscan priest here. I think he was a Franciscan. Well, whatever....He preached at one of the Sunday Masses here. He was a visiting priest. We never saw him before or after. I think he was here for the wedding of a nephew the day before and the pastor asked him to take one of the Sunday Masses. Well, he preached on the ability to say, 'Thank you.' And he simply suggested saying, 'Thank you,' for all the things people do for us everyday: holding doors, cooking, cleaning, delivering the paper, getting coffee, whatever. That's all he said—learning to say, 'Thank you.'"

I must have looked disappointed, because she added, "Yes, that was the best sermon I ever heard. It was short, simple and to the point. And guess what? For the past thirteen years my husband has been saying to me and all the people who do things for him, 'Thank you.'"

I still must have looked confused, so she added, "Oh, okay,

guess what? He never said 'Thank you' before he heard that sermon.''

Now that was a good sermon. Someone said something. Someone heard something. And that someone put it into practice. Imagine if that happened with every sermon: preachers saying something practical, people hearing the message, and then putting it into practice. We would have a changed world.

I said "Thank you" to the lady. I have thought about that sermon and that incident for the past few years. I have tried to say "Thank you" to those around me who do things for me. I certainly don't want to be dubbed, "The Man Who Never Said 'Thank you.' '' I have also worked on learning how to accept compliments and gratitude—knowing that I make mistakes, I can also learn from them.

A Theory

I have a theory. If we can't say, "Thank you" to each other for all that we do for each other each and every day, how can we say, "Thank you" to God?

I take my theory from lines that can be found in the Bible in the First Letter of John, where he says the following about love: "If anyone says, 'My love is fixed on God,' yet hates his brother, he is a liar. One who has no love for the brother he has seen cannot love the God he has not seen. The commandment we have from him is this; whoever loves God must also love his brother" (1 John 4: 20-21).

God is invisible. We are visible. So when we come to pray at the end of a day, how can we thank God if we didn't say, "Thank you" to our brother or sister that day? Or if we say, "Thank You" to God, how can those words mean anything if we never say, "Thank you" to the collector at the toll booth on the turnpike on a cold night, even though he or she is taking our money? Or when we go to a restaurant are we able to say, "Thank you" to the waitress (whether she is pretty or not), if the meal was good and the service was excellent? Would we stand there in the restaurant dining room an extra minute because our waitress or waiter was in the kitchen as we were leaving, so that we can say, "Thank you," catching the person's eye, in words and in person, and not just with a tip?

Hopefully, as we grow in our awareness and ability to say, "Thank you," we will grow in our appreciation for the interconnectedness of our world. We really do need to rely on each other. Why wait for a strike or a flood or a storm that knocks out the power lines to discover how much we rely on each other? The eye needs the hand and the head needs the feet, as St. Paul says. We are all parts of the one body (1 Corinthians 12: 20-21).

And as we grow in thankfulness for each other, we'll grow in our appreciation of God. More and more we'll begin to thank God for the sunrise and the sunset—for the beginning of a new day and the end of a long day. I still think God waits to hear, "Thank you" from us. I know I would.

Thank you for reading this book. I hope it helps you. Thirteen years from now, wouldn't it be great if you said, "Thirteen years ago I read something in a book about saying, 'Thank you' and I've been saying it ever since."

MANTRA: *"Thank you."*

47. THE MAN WITH THE TWO SUITCASES

ONCE upon a time there was a man who always traveled with two suitcases. Strangers thought it strange, but those around town, who knew him, got used to it.

He would show up at work, at stores, and even church—literally everywhere, with his two suitcases.

As I said, people around town got used to seeing him with the two suitcases. But what they never got used to were his cuts. He would often come to work with cuts all over his face and arms. "Suitcases, we're used to; cuts, now that is strange!"

The word was, "Don't ask him about the cuts. Don't ask him about the suitcases. And whatever you do, don't ask him what's inside the suitcases."

Whatever was inside seemed to weigh a lot, because he looked like he was carrying the world with him as he walked around with his suitcases.

Well, thank God, one day everything changed. It started in church. There he was sitting in the back and off to the side. He had a suitcase under each arm; he used them as armrests. The Gospel and the sermon that day were about, "The Woman Caught in Adultery." Nothing caught his attention, however, till he heard the word, "stone." "Let him without sin cast the first stone."

"Jesus is speaking to me," he thought. The priest in the pulpit said, "And Jesus said to the woman, 'Where did they all disappear to? Has no one condemned you?' 'No one sir,' she answered. Jesus said, 'Nor do I condemn you. You may go. But from now on avoid this sin' " (John 8: 1-11).

The man began to cry. It was a Fourth of July moment. The revolutionary war within him was about to end. Independence would be his.

After Mass, after everyone cleared out of the church, he walked up to the sacristy. Yes, he was still carrying both suitcases. "Can I talk with you, Father?" "Sure, what can I do for you?" "Well,

195

it's about these suitcases." "Yeah, I've often wondered just what you have in them, but I didn't want to embarrass you."

"Father, could we talk somewhere? I need to make a good confession." The priest brought him to a small room where they could talk. The man began by pulling out a key that was hanging on a string around his neck. He bent over and opened up one of the suitcases. It was filled with all kinds of rocks: little ones, big ones, sharp ones and flat ones.

The priest sat there silent. He had never seen anything like this before. Bag ladies, yes; but a suitcase man with rocks, no.

Then came the second surprise. The priest began to notice that each stone had ballpoint pen writing scratched on it. He began to read words, places and dates: "Tokyo—prostitute—June 16, 1973." "K-Mart Parking Lot—banged Chevy and ran—Jan. 28, 1987."

Inwardly, the priest yelled, "Oh no!" He caught himself, however, and after a few moments asked, "This is a collection of your sins, right?"

"Yes. I just can't get rid of them. I just can't let them go and they keep on driving me crazy. When I heard the Gospel and your sermon this morning, I realized that we all sin and if Jesus isn't going to throw stones at me, why should I be doing this to myself?"

Becoming very quiet, the priest wondered to himself: "Should I take him outside and the two of us bury the stones? Should we wash them, so the sins are washed off? Should we both take a trip to the river and toss them in? Maybe, if we washed them off, we could put them under the altar. It's wooden with a hollow inside. It would be a good reminder that he doesn't have to carry his sins any more. No, that would be dumb. The last thing in the world this man needs is to be reminded of his sins."

While the priest was musing on just what to suggest, the man spoke up. "All this is too much. Every time that I feel depressed or sorry for what I have done, I open up the suitcase, find the stone, and then bang myself in the head with it. I just can't seem to get rid of all these sins."

"What about the other suitcase?" the priest asked. "More sins?"
"Yes," the man answered. "But they are not my sins. Those are
the ways people have hurt me all through the years. They are
labeled and dated, too. I guess I just don't know how to let go,
to forgive and be forgiven, to forgive and forget."

The priest asked, "What do you want to do?"

The man was silent.

Finally, the priest broke the silence, "Do you want to go out
in the backyard, dig a hole, and get rid of all these rocks? Would
that help?"

"Listen, Father, this is what I would like. Could the two of us
go to the river? I know this is going to take a bit of time. I would
like to take each stone out of the suitcases, read it, then throw
it into the river. That's how I would like to confess this whole
mess."

"Ok, but I don't think Jesus wants you to go through all that
agony. I'll go to the river with you right now. We can use my
car. But, whatever you want."

The man sat there silently, thinking about what the priest said.
"No, I want to get rid of them one by one. That's how I collected
them and that's how I'd like to get rid of them."

MANTRA: *"Let him (her) without sins collect the first stone."*

48. WHATEVER HELP

I WOULD like to teach you two "new" prayers. Both are easy to say, but hard to put into practice, especially the first one. Both prayers consist of only one word. They are:

    1) "Whatever."
    2) "Help!"

When we are dealing with the struggles of life, sometimes we can do something to help the situation, and sometimes we are helpless. For example, we're caught in traffic. We scream, "Help!" We turn on the car radio to try to get a traffic report and perhaps find out what's causing the tie-up. We know there is an exit ramp a half-mile ahead. We inch our way up and get off there. We've done something. We've helped ourselves. At other times, we're just stuck. We don't know what happened and there is no exit ramp. That's when we have to learn to pray, "Whatever."

As you learn to pray both these prayers into your everyday life, you'll probably think that they must be the two oldest prayers around, because they are so basic.

Whatever

"Whatever" is the prayer of trust. It's the posture of letting go. It's saying to God, "Here, you take the car keys and do the driving. I just don't know what to do." It means saying to God, "I believe in you. I believe that whatever is happening right now is best for me and for all of us. I believe that you know what's going on, that you care for me, that you love me with unconditional love, and that you are involved in my life."

"Whatever" means letting go. We know what that means. We've all experienced moments of helplessness in our life. How many times in the past ten years have we heard people give the following advice for such moments, "Let go and let God." That's the "whatever" prayer in five words.

Look at the life of Jesus. His central vision was to do his Father's will. His constant prayer was, "Thy will be done." That's the "whatever" prayer in four words. In the garden, on the night before he died, Jesus wrestled with the wish of his Father. He saw himself as a chalice. He knew he was being hunted and would probably be killed. The chalice would be smashed. Who wants to go through that? He looked into the empty space of the chalice, the place for the Kingdom, the within. That was the important place, the empty space for the wine, the will of his Father. That's the only wine he could drink. And to have wine, grapes had to be crushed. And he had to walk that wine press alone. He wanted his disciples present, to be with him, to pray with him, but ultimately, he knew, he had to do it alone. "Thy will be done. Whatever."

And all of us at the end of our life must drink that same cup, and even if surrounded by family and friends, we will drink that cup alone. "Thy will be done." Others will scream and yell, "Help!" as we die, but we need to say, "Thy will be done. Whatever." In the garden, when Jesus was arrested, Peter drew his sword and struck the slave of the high priest, cutting off his ear. And Jesus said to Peter, "Put your sword back in the sheath. Am I not to drink the cup the Father has given me?" (John 18: 10-11).

Listen to the sayings of Jesus. He often talked about letting go— denying our very self and taking up the cross. He said to be careful that nothing and no one (mother, father, brothers, sisters, spouse, children, and possessions) get in the way of the Kingdom growing within us. The wheat seed must fall to the ground and die, otherwise it will never become wheat and bread. The grapes must be crushed, otherwise there will be no wine.

The field where the Kingdom must come is not out there. The field where the wheat and the wine must grow are in here. It's in "the me that's me." The "I" must die. The "me" must become a "we." No seeds planted, no wheat harvested. No grapes crushed, no wine flowing. Water that stands still is safe, but it stagnates. There is no Promised Land if we refuse to exodus from the slavery of Egypt. To receive, one must give. No cross, no crown; no pain, no gain; no Easter Sunday if there is no Good Friday.

This vision is the opposite of what we hear from all sides. We are a chalice. We are told to make the outside beautiful, to be a certain weight, to be a certain shape, to wear the right jewels and the right clothes. And we are told to fill the inside of the cup—the self—with stuff or with self-fulfillment, self-achievement, self-actualization, self-discovery, self-expression, etc.

Most of that can be good. It's important to eat right and get enough exercise. It's important to live life to the full and develop the self. The problems arise when we become so filled with self that we don't see our neighbor. The problems arise when we get caught up in externals. The problems arise when we start looking down on others because of their bodies or their clothes. The problems arise when we forget God as we search for self-fulfillment. The problems arise when we start measuring people by their titles, possessions, salaries, etc.

Jesus warned the Pharisees about cleaning the outside of the cup while the inside remained filthy and filled with sin. They got caught up in wanting to glitter and wanting to be noticed, "while neglecting justice and the love of God." (Luke 11: 37-54; Matthew 15: 1-20).

Isn't our prayer, "My kingdom come, my will be done, on earth as it is in heaven. Give me today my daily bread and forgive me my sins, even if I don't forgive those who trespass against me, and lead me not into situations that will harm me. Amen?"

The first step, then, in a deeper prayer life is to say to God, "Whatever." "Whatever you want, help me to want." "Thy Kingdom come. Thy will be done."

Help

I first learned of the "Help" prayer when I was reading *The*

Cloud of Unknowing, a classic written around 1370 in England, during the Hundred Years War and the Black Death. In chapter 37, the unknown author talks about the value of prayers that have very few words, "the fewer the better." He goes even further, advocating little words of one syllable as the best. And why? A person in a burning house does not yell out long sentences. They scream out words like, "Fire!" or "Help!"

"Help" is the prayer of the person who wants to get out of the hole. Don't just stand there, do something. Christianity not only teaches about surrendering when that is necessary, but it also teaches about fighting back, getting help. If we are stuck, we don't have to sit back and say, "whatever." We can scream for "Help!"

The Gospels are filled with stories about people screaming out for help. The blind man of Jerico yelled out, "Jesus, Son of David, have pity on me." He didn't want to spend the rest of his life blind if he didn't have to. "I want to see." A woman reached out to touch his garment to be helped. A centurian came to Jesus for his servant. A woman came for help for her daughter.

Jesus told us to ask, seek, and knock: "praying always and not losing heart." He told us to bother God till we get help. I've heard people criticize prayers of petition or begging prayers. I beg them to read the New Testament and change their mind. Be like the woman Jesus tells us about, who bothered a judge till he gave her a favorable judgment just to get her off his case. That's the way he told us to bother God (Luke 18: 1-8; Matthew 7: 1-7).

Prayer then is not an opium—a statement to oneself to give up and accept "whatever" happens. Karl Marx was right in his criticism of religion, when it is used to keep people passive. Prayer is a screaming out to God for "help," for justice, for wisdom to know what to do. Prayer leads us to gather with our neighbor and fellow workers to cooperate, to form unions, organizations, whatever the form of solidarity we can come up with to bring justice to all. God does not want to see his people falling down like a sagging fence or a battered wall (Psalm 61). God wants to help. God wants us to see a way out and make an exit, an exodus from slavery to freedom.

The Cross

Looking at the cross we can hear Jesus say the two basic prayers that I am reflecting upon in this meditation:

1) "Whatever": "Father, into your hands I place my spirit."
2) "Help!": "My God, my God, why have you forsaken me?"

The cross is the central symbol of Christianity. It can be seen everywhere: around necks, on walls, along highways and country roads, on top of churches. Some people still make the sign of the cross when they pass a church or come up to bat in baseball.

Philosophically, the Christian knows exactly what the cross means. Life consists of two ways: my way and the other way. I plan my day, my marriage, my family, my job, my life, one way, and then another way cuts aCROSS my way. The cross is as simple and as basic as that. As everyone says, "Life is what happens while we are making other plans." "Life is the interruptions." We hear the knock on the door, or the phone ring, and there has been a change in plans, or a car accident, or a fire or cancer.

Mysteriously, the Christian knows that the cross tells us so much more. The cross is not just two pieces of wood. There is a person on it. Our religion is a person. And that is why it's more than a philosophy and a system. It's a mystery. It's the story of a God who cares about the people he has created. It's the story of a God who helps. And it's the story of a God who suffers. Christ is God's statement, God's Word, that "I know you are there. I am not a God who sits back on a throne up there in the sky. No, I am a God who became flesh and lived among you." Our God is a

Liberator, a Redeemer, who entered into the very fabric of our life, and lived the whole cycle, from birth till death.

Jesus tells us that there are things in life that can be changed through HELP and there are things in life that cannot be changed WHATEVER we try to do. Going to Christ on the cross in prayer is a constant challenge to know which way to go. We look to Christ for the wisdom to know what can be changed and what cannot. We look to Christ for whatever help we can get.

MANTRA PRAYERS: 1) *Whatever.''*
                 2) *"Help!"*

49. HALF-DEAD AND THEN TO DIE

SOME people go through life half-dead and then they die. Isn't that stupid? We've all heard the statement that such people should have carved on their tombstones, "Died at 30. Buried at 60."

It must kill God to see us killing ourselves: killing time, rushing through meals without enjoying our food, working with our eye on the clock, dying for weekends and then wasting them on trivial pursuits, driving dangerously fast to get to some place where we sit around for hours doing nothing.

No wonder Jesus challenged us to live life to the full. No wonder Jesus was killed for making the life-giving statements that he made. No wonder Jesus cried over Jerusalem, seeing people sleep-walking, lost like sheep without a shepherd, wrapped in shrouds and wearing death masks. No wonder Jesus said from the cross that we don't know what we are doing.

I'm still waiting for someone to put a sign up at a football or a baseball game saying, "John 10:10." ("I came that you might have life and have it to the full.")

STOP! SLOW DOWN AND LIVE! SPEED KILLS!

Feel your pulse. If you have one, you're alive. Now, think about it: life is an amazing gift. Just what is it that keeps us alive? Certainly, it's not us. We have no control over whether we are going to die in five minutes. At least we know that a flashlight runs by battery and a lamp by electricity. If the batteries die or the electricity fails, the lights go out. But what makes us tick? What is it that makes us different from the body that is pronounced "dead" at the hospital? What is this amazing gift called "life" that hopefully we will have at 30, 60 and at 90?

Living with Passion

Three years ago, an old timer, aged 86, told me, "When I wake up in the morning, I wiggle my toes. If they wiggle back, then I say, 'Lord, thank you for another day. Help me to live this one to the full and to enjoy all the people you plan for me to meet and love today." He's still living full speed ahead.

We have all heard the joke: "First Man: 'How's your wife?' Second Man: 'Compared to what?' " We can ask: "How's your life?" And we can respond, "Compared to what?" Compared to so and so, I'm not too bad. But compared to so and so, I'm half-dead. We can ask further, "How's your everyday life? Married life? Family life? Sex life? Work life? Are your relationships life giving? Recreation life?" In other words, "How's your spiritual life?"

In a must-read book on this topic of being very much alive, see *Mystical Passion* by William McNamara. He subtitles the book, "Spirituality for a Bored Society." Listen to how he begins his first chapter: "Married lovers are not sexual and passionate enough. And what's more, neither are celibate lovers, who should be at least as sexual and passionate as married people. There is no other way to be a really great lover. And if religious men and women are not great lovers, what hope is there for Christianity?"

I live and work with young men who are thinking about becoming religious and priests. They notice everything. They meet people who are in "Religious Life" who are alive and they also meet some who are dead. After meeting a "doomsday" type, I heard one young man say, "How come he calls his death, 'Religious Life?' "

William McNamara would answer that young man by saying that the person had lost his passion. Nobody has a monopoly on death. You'll find dead people everywhere. As the old joke goes, "If you don't believe in the resurrection of the dead, be in classrooms, offices or factories when the signal is given for getting out."

For the sake of challenging you in this meditation about the quality of your life, I'd like to look at three specific areas:

1) Going to work,
2) Going to church—looking at priests,

3) Looking at the family—especially husbands and wives.

Going to Work

Every once and a while, "Dear Ann Landers" runs a clipping
called, "What is a Customer." Listen to its first four lines:
— "A customer is the most important person in any business.
— "A customer is not dependent on us. We are dependent on
    her or him.
— "A customer is not an interruption of our work. He or she
    is the purpose of it.
— "A customer is doing us a favor when he or she comes in.
    We aren't doing a favor by waiting on him or her."

"Yes!" We all respond to that—as long as we are the customer.
We see the log jams and the delays that the other person causes,
but not the ones we cause. Looking at what I do for a living: do
I give good service? Is the other person number two and I am
number one? Is my job life giving to others? Let's be honest. There
are people with three degrees who hate their job and are dead wood.
They sit around like an old alligator at the zoo. And there are people
with little or no "formal education," who rebuild motors or clean
office buildings, who love their job and find going to work a life-
giving experience.

Read the book *In Search of Excellence* by Thomas Peters and
Robert Waterman, Jr. It's all about motivation, creating a climate
for creative work, concern for customers, giving good service,
etc. I guarantee that if you read that book or listen to Tom Peters
on audio tape (available at shopping center bookstores), you'll go
to work with much more life than you did before reading the book
or listening to the tape.

I don't know about you, but I find toll collectors a lot friendlier
than other people who greet the public every day. They say
"Hello." They give directions. They take the beeps, the grunts
and the dirty looks from the people who follow the driver who

just got directions. It certainly has monotony, but I discovered more communication in them than in some priests in confession.

Going to Church—Looking at Priests

Speaking of priests, if there is one place all kinds of people complain about, it's going to church on Sunday. Dull sermons! Poor services! And the priest is usually the target of the criticisms.

Looking back at the many churches where I have preached, the strangest experience was in a place where everyone either looked down or off to the left. I preached there on three different occasions in the span of two years. All three times the congregation looked down or off to the left. Nobody looked at the pulpit or the altar. Outside of the church, after my third visit, a few people ventilated their anger and complaints about their "dead" pastor. He sped through the prayers of the Mass in monotone. He didn't allow for modern songs for the liturgy. He read his sermons. He never looked at anyone. The result was frustration, especially because the parish had lost a lot of its young people. That explained the looking down. But why did they look to the left? I asked about that and they laughed, because they didn't know they were doing that. The Blessed Sacrament altar was on the side they were looking at. Perhaps they were using their time at Mass to pray, instead of paying attention to their priest. I don't know to this day why they were looking to the left.

When does a priest die? When does he lose the fire and enthusiasm that moved him to enter the seminary with the hope of becoming a priest? When does his imagination dry up?

The Sunday sermon is the one moment each week when a priest can be spiritually creative and serve the majority of his parish. In connection with my job as novice director, I attended four workshops in the last month. Each was excellent, given by nationally known speakers in the field of initial and ongoing formation for religious and priests: Maria Rieckelman, Donna Markham, Ray Carey and Patricia Livingston. On all four occasions, the person who introduced the speaker said, "The speaker requests that tape recorders not be used to record the talks." I've yet to hear that on a Sunday morning. The gripe is that sermons are "canned," or unprepared, rehashed, half-baked, or left overs.

What would bring a priest back to life? An obvious answer would be to enter one of the many renewal programs that are around for priests and parishes. What are the factors that would wedge a "dead" priest into such a "resurrection" program? Should the bishops make this issue a national issue? It doesn't look like we are going to have women and/or married priests in the immediate future. Single and married "permanent deacons" are often neglected or rejected by both priests and laity. Having heard that so many priests have left the priesthood and those who stayed appear different or indifferent at the Sunday liturgy, it's no wonder that enough good people are not entering the seminary to become priests. I became a priest because I was impressed by the priests who asked me to think about becoming a priest. Today I've heard priests say they would never recommend that anyone become a priest. They make remarks like, "Our rectories have become wrectories."

Gripe! Gripe! Gripe! It sounds like I have a lot of gripes about priests, doesn't it? I do. They are the voices of people who have come up to me with a deep concern for our Church during the past 22 years that I have been a priest, and almost every time someone comes over with a comment—mostly negative—about a priest. I rejoice when I hear people brag about how great their parish and their priests are.

If you want to do something to improve the Sunday sermon, tell the preacher that you liked the sermon, if you liked it. A husband and wife recently asked me if there was a good book on sermon preaching that they could get for their priest. His sermons were poor. I suggested *Ten Responsible Minutes* by Joseph Manton C SS.R. It's published by Our Sunday Visitor, Inc., Huntington, Indiana 46750. Another book is *Preaching Better,* edited by Frank McNulty. It's put out by Paulist Press, 997 MacArthur Boulevard, Mahway, N.J. 07430. Frank McNulty quotes one of my poems in his book, but that's not the only reason I'm recommending it. Both books have good practical suggestions on how to improve a homily and both stress the main step: lots of hard work. Sermons take a lot of time and hard work.

Looking at the Family—Especially Husbands and Wives

We can ask the same questions of the married that we asked of workers and the clergy: When does the passion and the romance go? What renews the fire and the desire? How do we bring a dead marriage back to life?

When talking about the local church, I centered on the priests. Obviously that's being narrow and has been one of the problems we had in the past. However, I honestly think if the renewal isn't at the local clergy level, it's not going to be at the local parish level. I'm talking about tactics, more than theology. So, too, when talking about the family, the renewal must take place with wife and husband. Marshall McLuhan once said that marriages must be renewed every day. They also need to be renewed through more dramatic moments and programs. Thank God, for all the enrichment that has resulted from the Marriage Encounter Movement.

The next step is the putting together of the much richer theology of marriage that has been evolving from the married people of our Church. Since Vatican II we have a theology of marriage from theologians like Edward Schillebeeckx. What I am waiting to see is a national gathering of material on marriage from the married couples of our country. For starters, those who are giving Marriage and Engaged Encounters could copy their material and send it to a beginning committee. A pastoral on the economy and war and peace were put together. Now I would like to see the same model used for a national pastoral of marriage and the family. Married people have been telling us celibates for years that we just don't know the complete story. They sense that something has been missing in our sermons and presentations on Christian marriage. So I am seriously waiting for a much richer theology on marriage and family from the women and men of our Church who are living that experience.

In the meanwhile, for the sake of presenting something practical in this area of marriage and family, let me ask five questions. If you are married, I would suggest you do this exercise with your spouse. As in Marriage Encounter, write down your reflections before discussing them.

1) What do you see missing in the theology and spirituality of marriage that you hear from the pulpit and the Catholic press? Have you heard any new voices? What are they saying?

2) Do you take time out on a regular basis for clear communication with your spouse? In other words, do the two of you sit down once a week and ask each other, "How's it going? Feelings? Gripes? Suggestions? Future plans?"

3) Is your partner still central? Or have the kids, a job, an organization, another person, replaced your spouse as central?

4) With regards to your kids, are you living vicariously? In other words, are you living their life instead of your own? Are you pushing your children to become successful because you weren't? We have all heard of parents at Little League games taking the games more seriously than their kids. Are you putting any pressure on your kids about college, jobs, the person they marry, the way they must have the marriage ceremony, the kind of wedding reception they must have, where they are to live, how their kids should be raised, etc.? Or take the issue of going to church. Many people go to church for years to please their parents. Then they drop out for a few years. They have kids and start going to church to

give good example to their kids. Do you ever go to church because you want to go to church, regardless of your parents or your children?

5) When was the last time you surprised your spouse with a gift or a sign of your love that totally rocked them in their socks or pantyhose?

MANTRA: *"I have come that you might have life and have it to the full."*

50. LOVE IS OUTSIDE THE NUMBERS

LOVE is outside the numbers.

Once people who love each other start counting, then something has died.

"I took the garbage out three times last week and you haven't taken it out in the past two weeks."

"Who's counting?"

"I emptied out the dishwasher every morning this week and you haven't done it once."

"Who's counting?"

"I helped with the kids' homework at least a dozen times this new school year and I haven't seen you do it yet."

"Who's counting?"

"But we made love three times this week already."

"Who's counting?"

"Three times in a row now you finished the toilet paper roll and didn't replace it with a new one."

"Who's counting?"

"Mom, that's the third time this evening that you said, 'Where's my pocketbook?' You must be getting senile."

"Who's counting?"

"I got up to answer the phone three times already this evening and you haven't gotten up once."

"I didn't know we were counting."

Peter came up to Jesus and asked, "Lord, when my brother wrongs me, how often must I forgive him? Seven times?" (Matthew 18:21).

And Jesus answered, "Who's counting?"

"Two men went up to the temple to pray: one was a Pharisee, the other a tax collector. The Pharisee, with head unbowed, prayed in this fashion: 'I give you thanks, O God, that I am not like the rest of men—grasping, crooked, adulterous—or even like this tax collector. I fast twice a week. I pay tithes on all I possess' " (Luke 18:9-14).

And God said, "Who's counting?"

"When those hired late in the afternoon came up they received a full day's pay, and when the first group appeared they supposed they would get more; yet they received the same daily wage. Thereupon they complained to the owner, 'This last group did only an hour's work, but you have put them on the same basis as we who have worked a full day in the scorching heat.' 'My friend,' he said to one in reply, 'I do you no injustice. You agreed on the usual wage, did you not? Take your pay and go home. I intend to give this man who was hired last the same pay as you. I am free to do as I please with my money, am I not? Or are you envious because I am generous?' Thus the last shall be first and the first shall be last" (Matthew 20:1-16).

"Who's counting?"

"In your prayer do not rattle on like pagans. They think they will win a hearing by the sheer multiplication of words" (Matthew 6:7).

"Who's counting?"

And Peter told Jesus that he was hurt when he asked him three times, "Do you love me?" (John 21:15-19).

And Jesus said, "Who's counting? Do you love me?"

MANTRA: *Love is outside the numbers.*

51. SPIRITUALITY: WHAT HAPPENS WHEN YOU WALK INTO A ROOM?

WHAT happens when you walk into a room?

Did you ever ask yourself that question? When you raise your hand to say something? When people see you walking towards their car? When you are headed towards someone's front door? What reactions do you cause? What do people say about you under their breath?

Is it an "Oh, yes" or an "Oh, no" vote?

Or is the vote still out? Are people still thinking about you, still experiencing you, still saying inwardly and probably unconsciously, "Keep talking. One of these days I'll cast my vote for or against you!"

Will it be an "Oh, yes" or an "Oh, no" vote?

Obviously, people can miss and make mistakes about us. They might vote by hearsay. We might remind them of their fourth grade teacher or their mother. If we wear a uniform, that, too, might trigger different reactions. Presidents, governors, senators, all those who run for office are told by specialists how to *Dress for Success* and how to dress for votes. Lawyers tell their clients what color and the kind of clothes to wear in the courtroom. We judge books by their covers.

But what about those who know us? Those are the people to think about. What's their vote on us? Is it an "Oh, yes" or an "Oh, no" vote?

Spirituality

For the past ten years I have wondered about the word "spirituality." I was hoping to understand just what the word meant. I found a dozen good definitions. However, no one definition grabbed me. I don't like long, abstract definitions. I don't like definitions with "dictionary" words. I try to go by the KISS principle: "Keep It Simple, Stupid."

So I gave up trying to come up with a good definition for the word "spirituality." In the meanwhile, the word kept appearing in combinations with other words:

— Jewish Spirituality,
— Jesuit Spirituality,
— American Indian Spirituality,
— The Spirituality of Marriage,
— The Spirituality of John of the Cross,
— The Spirituality of Julian of Norwich,
— Traditional Spirituality,
— Modern Spirituality,
— Post-Vatican II Spirituality.

Then it struck me: why not use the word "spirit" instead? Why not think of spirituality as the spirit we emit? When you walk into a room, what kind of a spirit do you give off?

For example, if you studied the life of St. Francis, if you prayed over the Gospel texts that he lived by, if you integrated that spirit into your life, hopefully then, when you walked into a room, you would give off the spirit of Francis. You would have a Franciscan spirituality.

That made sense to me. More and more I began to see the word "spirit":

— Team spirit,
— Community spirit,
— School spirit,
— "She has a nice spirit,"
— "We need more people around here with a
   spirit of sacrifice."

Each of us has a spirit within us. Each of us has a spirit that we give off. That's our spirituality. It's the buildup and the integration of all the experiences of our life. God breathed into us the gift of life. So too have all the people whom we have met so far. Everything molds us: television, parents, brothers and sisters, where we are in the birth order, the books we read, the schools we attended. "Show me your friends and I'll tell you what you are."

Spirit is invisible. But we know what school or family spirit looks like. Each of us has one. We give it off as soon as we walk into a room. Others catch it. It's like a perfume or a spray from a deodorant. The question is: what kind of a spirit do I give off? Is it joy or pain, happiness or sadness? Do I uplift or dampen it? Do people say of me: "She has such a nice way about her?" Or do they say, "He's an angry young man?"

And that spirit that we have within us is powerful. It can go through walls. It can travel at the speed of thought. A woman told me she was on vacation in July and someone mentioned "Christmas." She immediately found herself tightening up and saying, "Oh no!" She knew that Christmas meant mother was coming to town and mother meant two weeks of nagging tension.

When someone mentions your name at a party or a get together, what reactions does your name set off? Are others indifferent towards you or do they give you an "Oh, yes" or an "Oh, no" vote?

Baby

There is one moment in our life when we almost always get an "Oh, yes" vote. It's when we were babies. People saw us and said, "Wow!" or "Oh yeah!" They were amazed at us. They stopped to spend time with us.

Haven't we all come around the corner in the supermarket and there in the aisle was this beautiful baby in a shopping cart smiling at us? Didn't we say, "Wow!" at it? The baby's spirit got to us.

Thirty Years Later

Thirty years later there is that same baby sitting across from us at a meeting. She is driving us crazy with her talking on and on and on. And inwardly we are giving her an "Oh, no" vote.

Why do beautiful babies become difficult people? Why do people change? Somewhere in some book I saw two pictures. I think they were on the same page. One picture had a tableful of beautiful smiling babies. The picture below it showed a subway car of people. Some were sitting. Some were standing. None were smiling. And underneath the subway picture were the words, "What happened?"

What Happened?

There are two basic reasons why people lose their "Oh, yes" vote for an "Oh, no" vote:

First of all, it's the fault of others. People in our life got tired of us. Our parents stopped "wowing" us. They got tired of being interrupted while reading the paper or taking a nap. They stopped reading stories to us. They put us in front of a TV to keep us busy. They stopped listening to us. They lost interest in us. One of our parents or both of them had a tough day at work and they found it difficult to be present to us. They couldn't shake things that were happening at the office. Then there are the horror stories—when kids were neglected or abused. The reasons are in the hundreds—from teachers who were just doing a job, to parents who were sick and tired of being a parent.

Secondly, it could be that we started to negate ourselves. If those around us were doing it, we might as well join in the fun of making fun of ourselves. The vicious cycle of negative thinking and behavior took over running our life. When we talked we began putting our hand to our mouth. Who is interested in what we have to say anyhow? We looked at ourselves and only saw a "dull" person. We gave ourselves an "Oh, no" vote.

"Help!"

What do we do to change the vote?

In the last 25 years there has been an overabundance of "self-help" books. Evidently, a lot of us had a poor self-image. Pre-

Vatican II spiritualities did not put much stress on self-value. Read *The Imitation of Christ* and it gives off an "Oh, no" vote for the individual.

Think back to the books and the sermons of the 1960's and 1970's. The stress was on self-value and a healthy self-love. All those books and tapes by John Powell are still worth listening to. Catch his spirit. He's giving a breath of fresh air to our way of looking at ourselves and others. One of my favorite books is still available in book stores, *"I ain't much, baby—but I'm all I've got."* It's by Jess Lair. Haven't we all improved in this area of self-acceptance in the last 25 years?

Solutions

What's the solution? Besides self-help books and tapes, we can take the road to recovery by looking at the same two ways—but in reverse—that people become negative in the first place: through self and others.

First, we need to begin with ourselves. Jesus told us to look within. Start with our own "I" first. Stop and ask yourself: "Honestly, am I an 'Oh, yes' or an 'Oh, no' vote? Am I happy to be me?" If I answer negatively, then what am I going to do for help? The solution is not to try to become another person. "Be who you is, because if you be who you ain't, then you ain't who you is." Society and the whole commercial world are pushing all kinds of products on us that promise to get us "Oh, yes" votes. The solution isn't out there. Don't we know down deep that the answer is there? We know how to get "Oh, yes" votes. We go to God and hear God speak to us, "And everyone I make is good." We go to the Lord in prayer and ask him to remake us, forming us anew, breathing into us his own Spirit.

Secondly, we begin to forget ourselves and love others. We go around giving others "Oh, yes" votes, because we believe that everyone the Lord creates is special. We exist for a reason.

One powerful way to give another an "Oh, yes" vote is to listen to them. Listening is magic. It's a way of saying to another, "I know you exist and you're worth listening to." Listen to any conversation. We don't listen. A says something about a recent vacation to Hawaii. B, hearing the word "vacation," jumps in when A stops to breathe, to tell about her recent vacation to Europe. C then talks about his new German car because the word "Europe" triggered the words "German car." Imagine if B asked A about the best part of her vacation in Hawaii and really was interested and listened. And imagine if C asked A about the kinds of gifts one can pick up in gift shops in Hawaii. Wouldn't A's spirit soar as B and C responded with questions to her comments, rather than comments about their interests? Aren't we all into monologues? To listen better, all we have to do is forget and deny ourselves and listen to the other person's story, instead of babbling about our own stories.

By becoming aware of the other person, by giving them an "Oh, yes, you're worth listening to" vote, they slowly change their negative vote about themselves to a more positive vote. Then people become more interesting. People will begin wanting to eat with them. I've noticed that whenever I ask people questions about what they are talking about, their eyes sparkle. Then, almost always, having been listened to, they begin to realize that another is present. They stop and say, "I've been doing all the talking. What about you?" When we listen to people, when we are really present to them, they become less self-centered. Their spirit is renewed. They begin to ask questions and listen to what we have to say. Don't we all feel great when someone listens to us? Don't we inwardly say, "Oh, yes!"

What happens when you walk into a room? It doesn't have to be a negative vote.

MANTRA: *Come holy Spirit! Help me to send forth your spirit when I walk into a room.*

52. I GUESS I'M LIKE EVERYBODY ELSE

"I guess I'm like everybody else."

I don't know how many times I have heard people blurt out those six words. But I've heard them loud and clear on retreats, in small groups, on the stairs, in spiritual direction, on the bus, over the phone and dozens of other places and situations.

"I guess I'm like everybody else."

And I wonder if I'll ever stop saying them to myself. One of the gifts of listening to other people's stories is hearing one's own story over and over and over again.

Do Dear Abby or Dear Ann Landers ever get surprised anymore?

Lately, when people say, "I guess I'm like everybody else," I find myself responding, "Welcome to the human race."

If the 70's was the so called "Me Generation," then the 80's is the "We Generation."

We would like to be unique and special, but we are learning more and more that we are dependent upon each other. No one is an island. Robinson Crusoe was scared when he saw another's footprint. He wasn't ready yet to say, "Thank God, it's Friday." It takes time to get used to other people, especially if we haven't gotten ourselves together yet. Every married couple knows that. But if we don't learn to work together, we're not going to make it individually or as a family.

That's why we need to listen to each other's stories. That's why we need to look at each other's footprints. We are quite similar. We often walk the same paths.

Isn't that the secret of Alcoholics Anonymous meetings? Someone gets up, tells their name, says they are an alcoholic, and then tells their story. And in that telling, we also hear our story. And when we cry, we know we are home.

Isn't that the secret of a good movie, novel, song or play? We see ourselves as in a mirror. "They're playing our song." And when we cry, we know we are home.

Isn't that the strength of the story of Jesus? We are the blind man; we are the woman caught in adultery; and we are Nicodemus coming with questions in the night. If Jesus could enter into their story, he can enter into our story. And when we cry, we know we are home. "Amen. Come Lord Jesus." "Lord, that I might see."

Hopefully, this book has helped you hear your story and make you feel at home. Hopefully, as I made footprints in the field of spirituality, you were able to see steps that you could take. As stated earlier in this book, I didn't plan this book to be autobiographical. As I went along with the writing, parts of my story came out. I hope you said, "I guess I'm like everybody else."

Before I end this book, I want to thank Joel Wells again for asking me to write this book. Having written several books himself, he understood when I fell behind schedule. "I guess I'm like everybody else." Thanks too, for Mrs. Barbara Feeney, our secretary here at the Mount. She took my handwritten meditations, typed them into a word processor, and then re-did all my corrections, Without her help, it would be a few more months before I could say, "Thank God, it's Friday"; this book is finally finished. Ever had that feeling of finally finishing something?

MANTRA: *"I guess I'm like everybody else."*